Rand Hummel

Gratefully Yours

+ + + + +

journeyforth®

Greenville, South Carolina

Library of Congress Cataloging-in Publication Data
Hummel, Rand, 1956–
  Gratefully yours / Rand Hummel.
    p. cm.
  Summary: "A review of Romans and the ways we can be grateful for our
salvation"—Provided by publisher.
  ISBN 978-1-60682-389-7 (perfect bound pbk. : alk. paper)
  1. Bible. N.T. Romans—Criticism, interpretation, etc. I. Title.
  BS2665.52.H86 2012
  227'.107—dc23
                                                              2011052637

Design by Nathan Hutcheon
Page layout by Michael Boone

© 2012 by BJU Press
Greenville, South Carolina 29614
JourneyForth Books is a division of BJU Press

Printed in the United States of America
All rights reserved

ISBN 978-1-60682-389-7
eISBN 978-1-60682-454-2

15   14   13   12   11   10   9   8   7   6   5   4   3   2   1

*To my wonderful wife Amber.
I couldn't do what I do without her.*

CONTENTS

Introduction

I beseech you therefore, brethren, by the mercies of God, that ye present your bodies a living sacrifice, holy, acceptable unto God, which is your reasonable service. *(Romans 12:1)*

How many things does a person have to know to live and die a happy, contented, and fulfilled life? Bible scholars and Bible students have wrestled with this question for centuries and the general consensus seems to be only three: (1) how great are my miseries and sin; (2) how I can be delivered from my misery and sin; (3) how I am to be thankful to God for such deliverance.

When Paul wrote the word *therefore*, he was not just giving a general glimpse of the three hundred fifteen verses of Romans 1–11, but specifically man's complete ruin in sin (Romans 1–3) and God's perfect remedy in Christ (4–11). Knowing what we were and what God has done, should it not impact the way we live each day?

Strong Bible teaching should always be accompanied by solid Bible application. Doctrine without application could give us big heads and little hearts. Application without doctrine could result in full hearts and empty heads.

It is not difficult to understand the extreme wickedness of our own hearts, but to clearly explain what God has done for us and why He would treat such wicked sinners with such love? Now things get difficult. The end of Romans 11 reveals to us how untraceable and unsearchable God's deliverance, mercy, and grace to us really are.

Enjoy your personal inspection of Romans 12 and of the twenty-four ways you can say "Thank You!" to a God Who has done so much for you.

Overwhelmed with what God has done for me,
Rand Hummel

SECTION 1

Man Has Ruined His Life in Sin

ROMANS 1–3

+   +   +

CHAPTER 1

Man Has Completely Ruined His Life in Sin

ROMANS 1

"Lord, do I truly understand the depth of depravity
and the extreme wickedness of my own heart?"

Paul starts out his personal letter to a group of young
Roman believers by painting a very dark picture of man's
heart. Man has completely ruined his life in sin. Man is
innately wicked with a bent toward evil. In his first few
paragraphs written to those living in Rome, Paul's inspired
teaching refutes the false philosophies of many humanistic
psychologists and well-meaning religious leaders. Man is not
innately good, but definitely evil and in dire need of a savior
who can save him from the natural and eternal consequences
of such evil. Four times Romans 1 gives a general indication
of what man is really made of. This is not (and never will be
aside from God's deliverance) a pretty picture.

*For the wrath of God is revealed from heaven against all
ungodliness and unrighteousness of men, who hold the truth
in unrighteousness.* (Romans 1:18)

Because that, when they knew God, they glorified him not as God, neither were thankful; but became vain in their imagi nations, and their foolish heart was darkened. (Romans 1:21)

Who changed the truth of God into a lie, and worshipped and served the creature more than the Creator, who is blessed for ever. Amen. (Romans 1:25)

Who knowing the judgment of God, that they which commit such things are worthy of death, not only do the same, but have pleasure in them that do them. (Romans 1:32)

Paul begins his portrait of a wicked heart in verse 18: "For the wrath of God is revealed from heaven against all ungodliness and unrighteousness of men, who hold the truth in unrighteousness."

The wrath of God has been and will continue to be revealed from heaven against all ungodliness and unrighteousness of men who suppress or hold the truth down by their wickedness. Did it ever occur to you that God gets angry? Why? What is so important to God that it would actually cause Him to unleash His wrath? Answer: Ungodliness and unrighteousness. When men give their sin (unrighteousness, wickedness) free reign, they are choosing to push God, and the truth about God, totally out of their hearts, minds, and lives. They know better! (And so do we.) Ignoring what God has said is like holding an inflated balloon under water—the truth cannot be hidden for very long before it pops back up and reveals how wicked we really are. The reason that God hates sin so much is that He loves us so much. Sin is the great separator. Those who reject God's loving forgiveness will be separated from Him for eternity.

Every opportunity to excuse such wickedness is erased as Paul continues in Romans 1:20b–21, "They are without excuse: because that, when they knew God, they glorified Him not as God, neither were thankful; but became vain in their imaginations, and their foolish heart was darkened."

They are without excuse. These guys knew better but chose to ignore and look down upon God. They are without excuse. The opposite of glorifying God is actually blaspheming God. Their incredible love for sin created an overwhelming hatred for God. They are without excuse. Matthew described the same kind of empty, dark thinkers of Romans 1:21 when he wrote: "No man can serve two masters: for either he will hate the one, and love the other; or else he will hold to the one, and despise the other" (Matthew 6:24). We will either love God and hate sin or love sin and hate God. There is no middle ground. People bent on wickedness will be loyal to (hold to) their sin and despise God by treating Him as worthless, irrelevant, and unnecessary—a scary place to be.

To justify their own sin, these guys started thinking up foolish ideas of what God was like. A loving, forgiving, holy God was not good enough for them because such a God would hold them responsible for their sin. So they had to make up their own pretend god. It is pretty foolish (even stupid) to make a pretend god in your own image. If you really were bent on stealing, cheating, and lying, what kind of pretend god would you make up in your mind? These guys "changed the truth of God into a lie, and worshipped and served the creature more than the Creator, who is blessed for ever. Amen" (Romans 1:25). Idolatry is an ancient form of self-worship. Men made up pretend gods that would allow them to do whatever they wanted to do. These gods were self-serving gods. Evil men twisted God's Word to say what they wanted it to say, which gave them permission to worship and serve themselves. Sound familiar? You do not have to look far into our media or sports world of superstars to find those who seem to be worshipping themselves instead of God.

At whatever point our wicked, depraved hearts ignore or even mock an all-knowing, ever-present God, we are in trouble. "Who knowing the judgment of God, that they which commit such things are worthy of death, not only do the same, but have pleasure in them that do them" (Romans 1:32). Can you imagine defending yourself before a judge who was there when you committed the crime, and knows not only what you did, but also why you did it (your entire thought process)!

We can choose our sin but not its consequences. According to Romans 6:23, most of us know what the ultimate consequence (wage or payment) of sin is. As a sinner, I deserve to die! And so do you. Some not only choose to sin themselves, but find pleasure in others who sin—giving hearty approval by paying to be entertained by it. The excuse, "I'm not the one doing it!" while watching sinful acts onscreen or online won't cut it before God. Finding pleasure in others who live in sin has become the basis for most entertainment plots in popular movies and current TV today. What do you do to protect yourself from such entertainment?

Those who ignore God's Word and push it out of their lives will soon ignore God and push Him out of their lives; they will worship themselves as their own gods and will receive what they ask for: a life *without* God—without God forever and ever.

CHAPTER 2

Does God Ever Give Up on Man?

ROMANS 1

"Lord, does there come a point when You give up on men and let them receive the consequences of their sin?"

There are three phrases (the first one repeated) that should cause unbelievers to shudder and tremble in their boots. Even though this is not what God desires (He is "not willing that any should perish" [2 Peter 3:9] and finds "no pleasure in the death of the wicked" [Ezekiel 33:11]), He inspired the following words of hopelessness and helplessness for all to see and read. The ultimate statement of God's wrath is not found in chastisement or correction; it is sadly observed when God gets quiet.

Wherefore, God also gave them up . . . (Romans 1:24)

For this cause, God gave them up . . . (Romans 1:26)

God gave them over . . . (Romans 1:28)

For the wrath of God is revealed from heaven against all ungodliness and unrighteousness of men, who hold the truth in unrighteousness. (Romans 1:18)

Don't push God to the edge... he will let you so on by YOURSELF

7

We cannot compare the wrath of God with the wrath of men. Our anger is often selfish, out-of-control, emotional, and foolish. God's wrath is motivated by and wrapped up in love. It is because of His extreme love for us, and His infinite knowledge of how sin can impact our relationship with others, our relationship with Him, and our eternity, that His wrath is revealed against all ungodliness and unrighteousness. When people refuse to listen and repeatedly tell God to leave them alone, there comes a time when God does what they ask for and stops convicting them. When God gets angry, He does not yell and scream. He just gets quiet.

Wherefore God also gave them up to uncleanness through the lusts of their own hearts. (Romans 1:24)

Because these Romans 1 men and women chose to love their sin and ignore God, God gave them up! Another way of saying this is that God "gave them over to" what they craved and desired. They did not want God. They did want sin. God simply gave them what they wanted, desired, and lusted after—uncleanness. When people allow their fleshly desires to become their gods (and the true God steps back and allows them to have what they want) they are reducing themselves to the point of acting like nothing more than animals. You don't have to spend much time on a farm to realize that most hogs (whether a sire, a sow, or a cute little piglet) love to get dirty. They find joy in uncleanness. Sadly, many men and women love to wallow in their own lustful filth. This is sad.

There is something incredibly refreshing about being clean. What is the first thing you want to do after a long road trip, a three-hour sports practice, or a hard day at work? A nice hot shower. It is too bad that we don't look at our inward cleanliness in the same way. Physically we don't like to be dirty. Can you say the same thing about your spiritual life? Immoral sin will make you feel dirty; God's forgiveness will make you completely clean. Violating a few simple commands from God's Word can begin to cover the heart with a kind of filthy dust that can soon desensitize it from all feeling;

God's undeserved grace cleanses us from all (that means *all*) unrighteousness. If you are like me, you have to agree with what King David, the apostle John, and the apostle Paul shared for all of us to read:

> *Who can understand his errors? Cleanse thou me from secret faults. Keep back thy servant also from presumptuous sins; let them not have dominion over me: then shall I be upright, and I shall be innocent from the great transgression. Let the words of my mouth, and the meditation of my heart, be acceptable in thy sight, O Lord, my strength, and my redeemer.* (Psalm 19:12–14)

> *I acknowledged my sin unto thee, and mine iniquity have I not hid. I said, I will confess my transgressions unto the Lord; and thou forgavest the iniquity of my sin. Selah. For this shall every one that is godly pray unto thee in a time when thou mayest be found.* (Psalm 32:5–7)

> *Hide thy face from my sins, and blot out all mine iniquities. Create in me a clean heart, O God; and renew a right spirit within me.* (Psalm 51:9–10)

> *If we say that we have no sin, we deceive ourselves, and the truth is not in us. If we confess our sins, he is faithful and just to forgive us our sins, and to cleanse us from all unrighteousness. If we say that we have not sinned, we make him a liar, and his word is not in us.* (1 John 1:8–10)

> *For this cause God gave them up unto vile affections.* (Romans 1:26)

To those who purposely chose to believe a lie about God (believing that He is not our sovereign Ruler who can make demands on our lives) and chose to worship the things that God created instead of the Creator God Himself, God "gave them over to" their degrading, shameful, immoral desires. They reduced their behavior to include sexual behavior that would not be natural for a squirrel, a bird, or even a hog. The word *perversion* could be used to describe sinful behavior that is a result of twisting and distorting God's words to give people permission to do what they wanted to do in the first place. We all have to ask ourselves if we do the same thing on a lesser scale. Is there anything in your life that you know is not best, but you justify or excuse it to keep it in your life? If so, from what we just learned, what should you do?

"And even as they did not like to retain God in their knowledge, God gave them over to a reprobate mind, to do those things which are not convenient" (Romans 1:28). Too many today live according to their likes and dislikes. Broccoli: If they don't like it, they don't eat it. Exercise: If they don't like it, they don't do it! Parents' rules: If they don't like them, they don't obey them. God's Word: If they don't like what it says, they ignore it and do what they want to do. The darkened hearts of the Romans 1 followers did not like to retain God in their knowledge. They ignored God and refused to acknowledge His presence, His power, or His preeminence over their lives. (Hopefully you do not fall into this same mindset.) Because of this, God "gave them over to" their empty, foolish thinking. They started doing what they were thinking! And what they did should have never been done. Think sin, then multiply it by ten, and you might get close to the depravity their foolish thinking led them to.

Even as believers, we have to guard our thoughts or we too will end up foolishly doing the foolish things that we foolishly think about. The word *reprobate* has the concept of being unworthy, unacceptable, unapproved, or undiscerning. I do not want even a hint of being reprobate in my heart, mind, or life. It is foolish to be foolish. So, when man foolishly gives up on God, does God ever give up on him? God is not willing that any should perish, but neither will He populate heaven with well-programmed robots or empty-headed puppets. When a man tells God, "Leave me alone!" God may just give that man what he wants and leave him alone . . . forever and ever.

CHAPTER 3

What Is the Extent of Man's Depravity?

ROMANS 1

*"Lord, please protect me from the long list of sins
that describes those who have foolishly chosen
to reject You and worship themselves."*

When Paul said, "God gave them over to a reprobate mind, to do those things which are not convenient" (Romans 1:28), he was simply saying that God gave them over to their depraved thinking, which resulted in a long list of inexcusable and sinful behaviors. Sad to say, most of the sins on the Romans 1 list are commonplace in our entertainment world, cyber world, and real world today (hopefully though, not in your world).

There are actually two lists in Romans 1:29–32. The first is centered on the phrases "being filled with" and "full of" and refers to the attitudes or thoughts of the heart. The second list starts with the last word of verse 29 (*whisperers*), continues through verse 32, and describes the actions of these Romans 1 God-haters. Paul is not coming up with something new here; Jesus expressed these same thoughts in Matthew 12:34–35 and again in Matthew 15:18–19.

O generation of vipers, how can ye, being evil, speak good things? For out of the abundance of the heart the mouth speaketh. A good man out of the good treasure of the heart bringeth forth good things: and an evil man out of the evil treasure bringeth forth evil things. (Matthew 12:34–35)

But those things which proceed out of the mouth come forth from the heart; and they defile the man. For out of the heart proceed evil thoughts, murders, adulteries, fornications, thefts, false witness, blasphemies: these are the things which defile a man: but to eat with unwashen hands defileth not a man. (Matthew 15:18–20)

Solomon also knew that although we are not what we think we are, we are what we think. What he penned in Proverbs 23:7 supports the teaching of both Paul in Romans and Christ in Matthew. "For as he thinketh in his heart, so is he" (Proverbs 23:7*a*).

Be warned of the extent of man's depravity and consider the consequence of each individual thought or action. The *attitudes* or "as he thinketh in his heart" could result in the list of *actions* or the "so is he". I want us to take some time and just think. Meditate. You don't have to write anything down, but let the Spirit of God stir your conscience with each question, explanation, and passage of Scripture. Don't forget—God is the One Who gave us this list.

How could unrighteousness impact my relationship with God and others?

- unrighteousness (what ought not to be; that which is unjust, wrong, and not right; discomfort with what is right and good)

But unto them that are contentious, and do not obey the truth, but obey unrighteousness, indignation and wrath, tribulation and anguish, upon every soul of man that doeth evil, of the Jew first, and also of the Gentile. (Romans 2:8–9)

How could fornication impact my relationship with God and others?

- fornication (any sexual sin, lewdness, immorality, perversion, moral uncleanness)

  But fornication, and all uncleanness, or covetousness, let it not be once named among you, as becometh saints. (Ephesians 5:3)

How could wickedness impact my relationship with God and others?

- wickedness (evil in nature, innate badness, utter depravity)

  And the Lord said unto him, Now do ye Pharisees make clean the outside of the cup and the platter; but your inward part is full of ravening and wickedness. (Luke 11:39)

How could covetousness impact my relationship with God and others?

- covetousness (greediness, the desire for more that is motivated by a discontented heart, the longing to have more and more of what God never intended us to have)

  And He said unto them, Take heed, and beware of covetousness: for a man's life consisteth not in the abundance of the things which he possesseth. (Luke 12:15)

How could maliciousness impact my relationship with God and others?

- maliciousness (evil, bad, a habitual wickedness rooted in the mind, evil from the inside out)

  Wherefore laying aside all malice, and all guile, and hypocrisies, and envies, and all evil speakings, as newborn babes, desire the sincere milk of the word, that ye may grow thereby. (1 Peter 2:1–2)

How could envy impact my relationship with God and others?

- envy (jealousy, being bothered to the point of thinking evil at the success and happiness of others, wanting what others have and not wanting them to have it)

For we ourselves also were sometimes foolish, disobedient, deceived, serving divers lusts and pleasures, living in malice and envy, hateful, and hating one another. (Titus 3:3)

How could murder impact my relationship with God and others?

- murder (slaughter; taking the life of someone for hateful, vengeful, or envious purposes; no respect for human life)

For from within, out of the heart of men, proceed evil thoughts, adulteries, fornications, murders. (Mark 7:21)

How could debating impact my relationship with God and others?

- debate (contention, argument, quarreling, strife)

For ye are yet carnal: for whereas there is among you envying, and strife, and divisions, are ye not carnal, and walk as men? (1 Corinthians 3:3)

How could deceit impact my relationship with God and others?

- deceit (baiting, tricking, or deceiving)

For he that will love life, and see good days, let him refrain his tongue from evil, and his lips that they speak no guile. (1 Peter 3:10)

How could malignity impact my relationship with God and others?

- malignity (evil-mindedness, thinking the worst of others, wicked disposition)

For this cause God gave them up unto vile affections. (Romans 1:26a)

Search me, O God, and know my heart: try me, and know my thoughts: and see if there be any wicked way in me, and lead me in the way everlasting. (Psalm 139:23–24)

CHAPTER 4

A Man's Thoughts Are an Index to His Character

ROMANS 1

"Lord, please protect me from my own selfish thinking.
I do not want to become a Romans 1 statistic."

A man's thoughts are an index to his character. What we think today we become tomorrow. The attitudes of our hearts often result in the actions of our lives. The depravity of our own hearts should cause us to shudder, fearing even the potential of our own wickedness. We must thank God for His daily provision of grace and mercy that keeps us from such depraved behavior. Romans 1:29–32 lists thirteen types of people who have given in to their depravity. By God's grace, may we never be accused of such actions or attitudes. As a man thinks, so is he. As you think, so are you! Take a few minutes and ask yourself if you could ever be accused of being a whisperer, a backbiter, a despiteful hater of God, a proud person, a boaster, an inventor of evil, a disobedient, undiscerning promise breaker, or an unloving, unforgiving, unmerciful person.

Could anyone accuse me of being a whisperer?
Whisperers are backbiting, malicious, secret slanderers. You

could call them lying gossips. The simple principle-based proverb, "Where no wood is, there the fire goeth out: so where there is no talebearer, the strife ceaseth" (Proverbs 26:20) still works.

Could anyone accuse me of being a backbiter? Backbiters are normally critical, insulting accusers. They are vicious tattletales. These are the ones that hang out on blogs and interact on the Internet, attacking and criticizing all those who, by their lives, are pricking their conscience and making them uneasy about their self-centered and selfish lives. They attack anyone who is not just like them and everyone who lives differently than they do. Peter nailed their character when he said, "They think it strange that ye run not with them to the same excess of riot, speaking evil of you: who shall give account to him that is ready to judge the quick and the dead" (1 Peter 4:4–5).

Could anyone accuse me of being a hater of God? Who would ever admit that they *hate* God except the Devil himself? Interesting enough, this term describes "haters of God" as "hiders from God." The concept is to abhor, to hate, to distance from, or to hide from. You cannot hide from God, and why would you want to? God told the prophet Jeremiah to write this simple question for all those who seek to hide from God: "Can any hide himself in secret places that I shall not see him? saith the Lord. Do not I fill heaven and earth? saith the Lord" (Jeremiah 23:24).

Could anyone accuse me of being despiteful? Do you know anyone full of spite? I doubt they are on your list of top ten friends. Despiteful people are often violent, arrogant, and insolent people who find some kind of meaningless satisfaction in attacking and persecuting others. Peter described them as those who "walk after the flesh in the lust of uncleanness, and despise government. Presumptuous are they, selfwilled, they are not afraid to speak evil of dignities" (2 Peter 2:10). Again, they are not the ones you would enjoy hanging out with.

Could anyone accuse me of being proud? Those who are ostentatiously proud try to look better than everyone around them. As they live their lives loving themselves and no others, they soon find that there are no others to love, since they have all been chased away by their selfish pride. One of the biggest problems with pride is the other attitudes that creep into the heart and fabric of the proud. Paul told Timothy that he would be dealing with men who would "be lovers of their own selves, covetous, boasters, proud, blasphemers, disobedient to parents, unthankful, unholy" (2 Timothy 3:2), and such men are usually too proud to change. Sad.

Could anyone accuse me of being boastful? Boasters are proud men. They are empty pretenders bragging about that which they do not possess or about accomplishing feats that they cannot accomplish. Paul took great care so that no one could accuse him or his friends of being proud or boastful. He reminded his young converts in Thessalonica when he wrote, "For our gospel came not unto you in word only, but also in power, and in the Holy Ghost, and in much assurance; as ye know what manner of men we were among you for your sake" (1 Thessalonians 1:5). You know who is proud and who is humble—just watch what they do and listen to what they say.

Could anyone accuse me of being an inventor of evil things? There are some who have so distanced themselves from God that they are consumed with and addicted to evil and are always looking and searching for ways to be involved in immoral wickedness. This is also part of a proud heart that chooses to love what God hates and hate what God loves. Solomon gave a list of seven things that God really hates in Proverbs 6. It is amazing how closely the list resembles some of the actions of Romans 1: "a proud look, a lying tongue, and hands that shed innocent blood, an heart that deviseth wicked imaginations, feet that be swift in running to mischief, a false witness that speaketh lies, and he that soweth discord among brethren." Instead we are to "let love be without dissimulation. Abhor that which is evil; cleave to that which is good" (Romans 12:9).

Could anyone accuse me of being disobedient to parents? This question of course is age sensitive, but we must never forget that a rebellious, defiant adult was once a rebellious, defiant child or teen who was never confronted or corrected with his selfish defiance. Any child, young or old, who would treat his mom or dad as if they were worthless has either a bitter heart, an angry heart, a guilty heart, or a hurting heart. Only foolish thinkers look down on, despise, or treat as dirt those in authority over them. Remember, "a wise son maketh a glad father: but a foolish man despiseth his mother" (Proverbs 15:20) and "the eye that mocketh at his father, and despiseth to obey his mother, the ravens of the valley shall pick it out, and the young eagles shall eat it" (Proverbs 30:17), signifying the kind of honor, respect, or even care these foolish thinkers will never experience in their lives.

Could anyone accuse me of being without understanding? A lack of understanding reveals a heart that has not learned to discern. In our world of high-tech information, there really are no excuses for lacking understanding. We have more tools at our fingertips than any generation before us. An afternoon of serious study should open our eyes not only to the consequences of most issues, but to the cause as well. Those who have no reasoning ability have literally chosen to have none. They would rather be handed a list than think through an issue. Most are more interested in the consequences of an action than in the understanding of why the behavior is good or bad, right or wrong, better or best. Unbelievers have no understanding and don't want any. Believers, not to the same extent, struggle with discernment on another level. The writer of Hebrews had to deal with those he worked with in a similar way.

> *Of whom we have many things to say and hard to be uttered,*
> *seeing ye are dull of hearing. For when for the time ye ought*
> *to be teachers, ye have need that one teach you again which*

be the first principles of the oracles of God; and are become
such as have need of milk, and not of strong meat. For every
one that useth milk is unskilful in the word of righteousness:
for he is a babe. But strong meat belongeth to them that are
of full age, even those who by reason of use have their senses
exercised to discern both good and evil. (Hebrews 5:11–14)

Could anyone accuse me of being a covenant breaker?
You cannot understand the import of a covenant breaker
unless you understand the importance of a covenant. When
a man and a woman take their marriage vows, they are
making a covenant, literally, a promise to be faithful to each
other. God has made many promises (covenants) with His
people, which He has never broken. Men who glibly break
their promises to either God or others are covenant breakers.
They are untrustworthy, undependable, and you cannot trust
what they say. There was a time when you could take a man
at his word with contracts, work agreements, loans, and even
relationships . . . no longer. Technically, someone who makes
a promise but has no intention of keeping that promise is not
only a covenant breaker but a liar. Solomon calls them fools
in Ecclesiastes 5:4: "When thou vowest a vow unto God, defer
not to pay it; for he hath no pleasure in fools: pay that which
thou hast vowed."

**Could anyone accuse me of being without natural
affection?** There are natural affections: the love between
a husband and a wife, the love between a mother and her
infant, or the love between a brother and a sister. We live in a
world where love for self has exceeded even the natural love
that should be for others. Because so many reject the love of
God, our world is filled with unloving and hateful people. A
husband who does not naturally love his wife files for divorce.
A young mother who does not naturally love the living baby
growing inside of her chooses to abort that child. A father
who does not naturally love his children verbally, physically,
and sexually abuses them. Parents who do not naturally love
their children reject them and abandon them to someone

else's care. This is not natural and not right. It is amazing how far a person who rejects God and chooses only to worship self can go. God's command in John 15:12–13 is the opposite of what you read in most daily newspapers today: "This is my commandment, That ye love one another, as I have loved you. Greater love hath no man than this, that a man lay down his life for his friends" (John 15:12–13). What a sad state of affairs our families, country, and world are in when people refuse to simply believe, trust, and obey God!

Could anyone accuse me of being implacable? Have you ever met an implacable man? If you have, you would know it. They are generally unforgiving, quarrelsome, and absolutely irreconcilable. Most implacables refuse to talk, reason, or forgive. If there is an issue at hand, you might as well talk to a telephone pole as to try to reason with an implacable person. We cannot change a person's heart, but as Paul reminds us, "If it be possible, as much as lieth in you, live peaceably with all men. Dearly beloved, avenge not yourselves, but rather give place unto wrath: for it is written, Vengeance is Mine; I will repay, saith the Lord" (Romans 12:18–19).

Could anyone accuse me of being unmerciful? The more self-centered a man becomes the less he offers mercy to others (and the more he will beg and cry for mercy someday). The more a person distances himself from God, the more unlike God he becomes. God is a God of mercy—He cares. The unmerciful have no compassion, no concern, and simply do not care about anyone or anything but themselves. Often, the more people have the less they give. John asks a very pointed question in 1 John 3:17: "But whoso hath this world's good, and seeth his brother have need, and shutteth up his bowels of compassion from him, how dwelleth the love of God in him?"

"Lord, please protect me from this long list of sins that describes those who have foolishly chosen to reject You and worship themselves. I do not want to become a Romans 1 statistic."

CHAPTER 5

Inexcusable Before God

ROMANS 2

"Lord, please keep me from the evils and the pitfalls
of both self-centeredness and self-righteousness."

Question: Are the good, moral people who reject God
            any better off than the wicked, immoral
            people who reject God?
Answer 1:   No. Both actually *do* what they know is sin
            in others.

*Therefore thou art inexcusable, O man, whosoever thou art
that judgest: for wherein thou judgest another, thou con-
demnest thyself; for thou that judgest doest the same things.
But we are sure that the judgment of God is according to
truth against them which commit such things. And thinkest
thou this, O man, that judgest them which do such things,
and doest the same, that thou shalt escape the judgment of
God?* (Romans 2:1–3)

If you attack someone who has offended you for being
harsh, unkind, and hurtful with a mean, unloving, critical
spirit, are you any better than they are? If you go on Facebook
and start a hate dialogue against someone who has secretly
slandered you, are you any better than they are? If you refuse
to forgive someone from your past, or won't even consider
meeting with them to reconcile your differences, are you any
better than they are? Even an outwardly moral person can be

21

a Romans 1:29–32 implacable whisperer or backbiter. Can you think of any attitudes in your own heart that could result in the actions that you hate in others?

Question: Are the good, moral people who reject God any better off than the wicked, immoral people who reject God?

Answer 2:   No. Both look down on God's kindness, forbearance, and patience.

Or despisest thou the riches of His goodness and forbearance and longsuffering; not knowing that the goodness of God leadeth thee to repentance? (Romans 2:4)

Too often we presume on the goodness of God. He is abundantly kind, incredibly tolerant, and inconceivably patient with each one of us! Too often we take this for granted. What if God gave us the same amount of kindness we give to others? What if God had the same level of tolerance toward our selfishness that we have toward those we live with? What if God lost His patience with us as often as we lose our patience with others? We would be in trouble.

Question: Are the good, moral people who reject God any better off than the wicked, immoral people who reject God?

Answer 3:   No. Both have hard, unbelieving hearts.

But after thy hardness and impenitent heart treasurest up unto thyself wrath against the day of wrath and revelation of the righteous judgment of God. (Romans 2:5)

This is a heart issue. The word *treasurest* means to store up in a safe place and, in this case, it is not gold (or even anything pleasurable) but the wrath of God that is being stored. God is patient! He is also just. Regardless of how religious a person is, if he chooses to reject Jesus Christ as Savior because of a stubborn (hard), unbelieving (impenitent) heart, he will someday experience the ultimate wrath of God unleashed. If you want to understand what those who reject Christ during the Tribulation years will experience, draw a mental picture of God's wrath as revealed in the bowls of wrath described in Revelation 16.

And I heard a great voice out of the temple saying to the seven angels, Go your ways, and pour out the vials of the wrath of God upon the earth. And the first went, and poured out his vial upon the earth; and there fell a noisome and grievous sore upon the men which had the mark of the beast, and upon them which worshipped his image. And the second angel poured out his vial upon the sea; and it became as the blood of a dead man: and every living soul died in the sea. And the third angel poured out his vial upon the rivers and fountains of waters; and they became blood. And I heard the angel of the waters say, Thou art righteous, O Lord, which art, and wast, and shalt be, because thou hast judged thus. For they have shed the blood of saints and prophets, and Thou hast given them blood to drink; for they are worthy. And I heard another out of the altar say, Even so, Lord God Almighty, true and righteous are Thy judgments. And the fourth angel poured out his vial upon the sun; and power was given unto him to scorch men with fire. And men were scorched with great heat, and blasphemed the name of God, which hath power over these plagues: and they repented not to give Him glory. And the fifth angel poured out his vial upon the seat of the beast; and his kingdom was full of darkness; and they gnawed their tongues for pain, and blasphemed the God of heaven because of their pains and their sores, and repented not of their deeds. And the sixth angel poured out his vial upon the great river Euphrates; and the water thereof was dried up, that the way of the kings of the east might be prepared. And I saw three unclean spirits like frogs come out of the mouth of the dragon, and out of the mouth of the beast, and out of the mouth of the false prophet. For they are the spirits of devils, working miracles, which go forth unto the kings of the earth and of the whole world, to gather them to the battle of that great day of God Almighty. Behold, I come as a thief. Blessed is he that watcheth, and keepeth his garments, lest he walk naked, and they see his shame. And He gathered them together into a place

*called in the Hebrew tongue Armageddon. And the seventh
angel poured out his vial into the air; and there came a great
voice out of the temple of heaven, from the throne, saying, It
is done. And there were voices, and thunders, and light-
nings; and there was a great earthquake, such as was not
since men were upon the earth, so mighty an earthquake,
and so great. And the great city was divided into three parts,
and the cities of the nations fell: and great Babylon came
in remembrance before God, to give unto her the cup of the
wine of the fierceness of his wrath. And every island fled
away, and the mountains were not found. And there fell
upon men a great hail out of heaven, every stone about the
weight of a talent: and men blasphemed God because of the
plague of the hail; for the plague thereof was exceeding great.*
(Revelation 16:1–21)

Question: Are the good, moral people who reject God
any better off than the wicked, immoral
people who reject God?

Answer 4: No. Both are *hearers* but not *doers* of God's
Word.

*Who will render to every man according to his deeds: to
them who by patient continuance in well doing seek for glory
and honour and immortality, eternal life: but unto them
that are contentious, and do not obey the truth, but obey
unrighteousness, indignation and wrath, tribulation and
anguish, upon every soul of man that doeth evil, of the Jew
first, and also of the Gentile; but glory, honour, and peace,
to every man that worketh good, to the Jew first, and also to
the Gentile: for there is no respect of persons with God. . . .
(For not the hearers of the law are just before God, but the
doers of the law shall be justified.)* (Romans 2:6–13)

Romans 2:6–11 reveals how important this truth is to
God. He states His concern in verses 6–8 and then repeats it
in verses 9–11. God is reminding us that He does not pick favorites; He blesses those who humbly obey and judges those
who stubbornly disobey. It's pretty simple to understand.
What does God promise to those who do evil? What does

God promise to those who do good? We choose whether we will receive glory, honor, and peace or wrath, indignation, tribulation and anguish. What is your choice?

Question: Are the good, moral people who reject God any better off than the wicked, immoral people who reject God?

Answer 5:   No. Both forget that they cannot keep secrets from God.

In the day when God shall judge the secrets of men by Jesus Christ according to my gospel. (Romans 2:16)

There is a day coming when God will judge the secrets of all men by Christ Jesus. Some are good at keeping a secret from others, and some tell the first person they meet. No one can keep a secret from an all-knowing, all-wise, omniscient God! God not only knows *what* you've done, He knows the motivation of your heart and *why* you did it. Some secrets are good! True servants serve God secretly, and no one knows but God. Some secrets are bad. Sinners who think they have sinned secretly will someday see that, with God, there are no secrets. What secret do you and God share that no one else on earth knows about?

Question: Are the good, moral people who reject God any better off than the wicked, immoral people who reject God?

Answer 6:   No. Both cause others to look down on God because of their wickedness.

For the name of God is blasphemed among the Gentiles through you, as it is written. (Romans 2:24)

When professing believers live in sin, unbelievers laugh. They laugh at both the sinner and the Savior. To blaspheme is to discredit with impious, irreverent words, or—as we would say today—to make God look weak, stupid, and irrelevant. The opposite of blaspheming God is to glorify God (1 Corinthians 10:31). Obedient, pure, godly lives glorify God as others see God empowering them to live holy, righteous lives in a wicked, God-hating world. So as your friends watch your life, do they glorify or blaspheme God?

Question: Are the good, moral people who reject God any better off than the wicked, immoral people who reject God?

Answer 7:   No. Both forget that a real relationship with God is a "heart" issue—not based on what they do, but on what they are.

For he is not a Jew, which is one outwardly; neither is that circumcision, which is outward in the flesh: but he is a Jew, which is one inwardly; and circumcision is that of the heart, in the spirit, and not in the letter; whose praise is not of men, but of God. (Romans 2:28–29)

Outwardly we can conform and perform in such a way that we look good. Paul is reminding us that a true believer is one inwardly, a person whose heart has been changed by God's Spirit and who by trusting Christ is willing to be identified with Christ, to live for Christ, and to depend on Christ and Christ alone for eternal life. It is not what we have done for Christ, but what Christ has done for us. What are you trusting in? Your goodness or God's grace? Your morality or God's mercy?

Question: Are the good, moral people who reject God any better off than the wicked, immoral people who reject God?

Answer 8:   No.

Therefore, thou art inexcusable, O man . . . Thinkest thou this, O man, that thou shalt escape the judgment of God? (Romans 2:1–3)

CHAPTER 6

Jesus Christ Is God's Remedy

ROMANS 3

"Lord, thank You for Your forgiveness!"

Romans 3 is one of the most convicting and comforting chapters of God's written Word. The first part of the chapter reminds me that I am a sinner. The final part reassures me that my sins have been forgiven by faith in Christ. It is good for me to be reminded of my sinful heart so that my expression of thanksgiving to God for His forgiveness may become a daily occurrence. Paul must have been thinking of Psalms 14 and 53 when God inspired him to write this nine-verse description of a depraved man's heart in Romans 3:10–18. The psalmist wrote:

> The fool hath said in his heart, There is no God. They are corrupt, they have done abominable works, there is none that doeth good. The Lord looked down from heaven upon the children of men, to see if there were any that did understand, and seek God. They are all gone aside, they are all together become filthy: there is none that doeth good, no, not one. Have all the workers of iniquity no knowledge? Who eat up my people as they eat bread, and call not upon the Lord. There were they in great fear: for God is in the generation

of the righteous. Ye have shamed the counsel of the poor, because the Lord is his refuge. Oh that the salvation of Israel were come out of Zion! When the Lord bringeth back the captivity of His people, Jacob shall rejoice, and Israel shall be glad. (Psalm 14:1–7)

The fool hath said in his heart, There is no God. Corrupt are they, and have done abominable iniquity: there is none that doeth good. God looked down from heaven upon the children of men, to see if there were any that did understand, that did seek God. Every one of them is gone back: they are altogether become filthy; there is none that doeth good, no, not one. Have the workers of iniquity no knowledge? Who eat up my people as they eat bread: they have not called upon God. There were they in great fear, where no fear was: for God hath scattered the bones of him that encampeth against thee: thou hast put them to shame, because God hath despised them. Oh that the salvation of Israel were come out of Zion! When God bringeth back the captivity of His people, Jacob shall rejoice, and Israel shall be glad. (Psalm 53:1–6)

In ninety-nine words, Paul describes the present heart of an unbeliever. Now remember, this is the former heart of all believers. If you trusted Christ as a small child, this describes what you would have become without Christ. None of us is beyond such depravity. We should be overwhelmed with thanksgiving and gratitude for God's mercy and grace that saved us from such depravity. So Paul gives us a list in Romans 3:11–18 of what we were or were going to become.

- There is none righteous, no, not one.
- There is none who understands.
- There is none who seeks after God.
- They have all turned aside.
- They have together become unprofitable.
- There is none who does good, no, not one.
- Their throat is an open tomb (sepulcher).
- With their tongues they have practiced deceit.
- The poison of asps is under their lips.

- [Their] mouth is full of cursing and bitterness.
- Their feet are swift to shed blood.
- Destruction and misery are in their ways.
- The way of peace they have not known.
- There is no fear of God before their eyes.

Romans 3:21 starts with the words, "But now," which Paul uses to transition from what was to what is; from what we were destined to be to what we have been made to be; from what we could have accomplished in the flesh to what God has accomplished by His grace. Let us never forget what God has done and continues to do on a daily basis. He forgives; He justifies; He redeems; (and the list could go on and on). So what has God done for us through Jesus Christ? Here are some wonderful truths to meditate on and to be thankful for.

But now the righteousness of God without the law is manifested, being witnessed by the law and the prophets. (Romans 3:21)

> God has shown us a way to be right with Him without fulfilling the requirements of the law as Moses and the prophets promised.

Even the righteousness of God which is by faith of Jesus Christ unto all and upon all them that believe: for there is no difference. (Romans 3:22)

> No matter who we are or what we have done, we are made right with God by placing our faith in Jesus Christ.

For all have sinned, and come short of the glory of God. (Romans 3:23)

> All of us have sinned and fall way short of God's glorious perfection.

Being justified freely by his grace through the redemption that is in Christ Jesus. (Romans 3:24)

> Unreservedly, through Jesus Christ, we have been freed from the penalty of our sin.

Whom God hath set forth to be a propitiation through faith in his blood. (Romans 3:25)

> God sent Jesus to be sacrificed for my sin—
> He shed His blood for me.

To declare his righteousness for the remission of sins that are past, through the forbearance of God. (Romans 3:25)

> God knew that Jesus would pay for sin and
> was just in holding off his punishment for
> those who sinned in the past.

To declare, I say, at this time his righteousness. (Romans 3:26a)

> God is fair, just, and righteous in the way
> that He deals with both sinners and their sin.

That he might be just, and the justifier of him which believeth in Jesus. (Romans 3:26b)

> God is always fair, especially in the way that
> He declares us sinners right in His sight as
> we put our faith and trust in Jesus Christ and
> Christ alone.

We have so very much to be thankful for. Romans 3 is one of the most convicting and comforting chapters of God's written Word. As we saw, the first part of the chapter reminds us that we are sinners. The final part reassures us that our sins have been forgiven by faith in Christ. It is good for all of us to be reminded of our sinful hearts so that our expressions of thanksgiving to God for His forgiveness may become a daily occurrence. He has given us much more than we deserve. Can you imagine what it would be like for all eternity if God actually gave us what we do deserve?

SECTION 2

God's Remedy Is in Jesus Christ

ROMANS 4–11

+ + +

In the first section of this book, we learned how depraved and wicked a man's heart can become when he refuses to listen to God and pushes Him out of his life. Just as darkness is defined by the absence of light and cold is defined by the absence of heat, so evil could be defined as the absence of God. When God is rejected and despised, evil reigns. The answer to such a wicked, depraved, sinful heart is the rescuing, redemption, and reconciliation through Jesus Christ. Romans 1–3 reminds us that man has ruined his life in sin; Romans 4–11 explains that God's remedy is in the death, burial, and resurrection of Jesus Christ. We are justified and sanctified in Christ and Christ alone.

No one can compile an outline quite like the outline guru Warren Wiersbe. In his famous *Bible Exposition Commentaries* (known better as the Be Series), he has organized eight lofty chapters into three main thoughts.

Using his outline and as few words as possible, we will attempt to get a solid overview of Romans 4–11 before we sink our minds into Romans 12. Remember, man ruined his life in sin but God's remedy is Jesus Christ. What God has done for us wicked sinners is simply amazing. Again, we should not let a day go by without thanking God for what He has done for us.

I. Salvation: Righteousness Imputed (Romans 3:21–5:21)

    A. Justification explained (Romans 3:21–31)

    B. Justification expressed: the example of Abraham (Romans 4)

    C. Justification experienced (Romans 5)

II. Sanctification: Righteousness Imparted (Romans 6–8)

    A. Our new position in Christ (Romans 6)

    B. Our new problem in the flesh (Romans 7)

    C. Our new power in the Spirit (Romans 8)

III. Sovereignty: Righteousness Rejected (Romans 9–11)

    A. Israel's past election (Romans 9)

    B. Israel's present rejection (Romans 10)

    C. Israel's future redemption (Romans 11)

CHAPTER 7

Justification Examined

ROMANS 4

jus·ti·fy (jŭs' tə fī), v.

1. To demonstrate or prove to be just, right, or valid.

2. To declare free of blame; absolve.

3. To free (a human) of the guilt and penalty attached to grievous sin.[1]

In Christian theology, justification is God's act of reckoning a sinner righteous before God by the imputation of Christ's righteousness.

As a sinner, I need forgiveness. Forgiveness is a promise (not a feeling) that my sin has been covered, dealt with, and forgiven so that it will not be brought up against me ever again. When God forgives, He justifies. When God forgives, He credits Christ's righteousness to my account. When God forgives, He frees me from the guilt and penalty of my sin. This forgiveness by justification is almost unbelievable, so that's where faith comes in.

> *For therein is the righteousness of God revealed from faith to faith: as it is written, The just shall live by faith.* (Romans 1:17)

> *Even as Abraham believed God, and it was accounted to him for righteousness.* (Galatians 3:6)

> *But that no man is justified by the law in the sight of God, it is evident: for, The just shall live by faith.* (Galatians 3:11)

> *And the Scripture was fulfilled which saith, Abraham believed God, and it was imputed unto him for righteousness: and he was called the Friend of God.* (James 2:23)

Romans 4 is all about Abraham. The Jewish community took a lot of pride in their ability to trace their linage back to this patriarch. Some even believed that by simply proving that they were direct descendants of Abraham they would be ushered into heaven—no questions asked. They thought they were safe because they were children of Abraham. In Matthew 3:1–6 and Luke 3:1–20, we read that John the Baptist dealt with this when he challenged the Pharisees and the Sadducees to prove by the way they lived that they had repented of their sins and turned to God.

> *In those days came John the Baptist, preaching in the wilderness of Judaea, and saying, Repent ye: for the kingdom of heaven is at hand. For this is he that was spoken of by the prophet Esaias, saying, The voice of one crying in the wilderness, Prepare ye the way of the Lord, make His paths straight. And the same John had his raiment of camel's hair, and a leathern girdle about his loins; and his meat was locusts and wild honey. Then went out to him Jerusalem, and all Judaea, and all the region round about Jordan, and were baptized of him in Jordan, confessing their sins.* (Matthew 3:1–6)

> *Now in the fifteenth year of the reign of Tiberius Caesar, Pontius Pilate being governor of Judaea, and Herod being tetrarch of Galilee, and his brother Philip tetrarch of Ituraea and of the region of Trachonitis, and Lysanias the tetrarch of Abilene, Annas and Caiaphas being the high priests, the word of God came unto John the son of Zacharias in the wilderness. And he came into all the country about Jordan, preaching the baptism of repentance for the remission of sins; as it is written in the book of the words of Esaias the prophet, saying, The voice of one crying in the wilderness, Prepare ye the way of the Lord, make His paths straight.*

*Every valley shall be filled, and every mountain and hill
shall be brought low; and the crooked shall be made straight,
and the rough ways shall be made smooth; and all flesh shall
see the salvation of God. Then said he to the multitude that
came forth to be baptized of him, O generation of vipers,
who hath warned you to flee from the wrath to come? Bring
forth therefore fruits worthy of repentance, and begin not to
say within yourselves, We have Abraham to our father: for
I say unto you, That God is able of these stones to raise up
children unto Abraham. And now also the axe is laid unto
the root of the trees: every tree therefore which bringeth not
forth good fruit is hewn down, and cast into the fire. And
the people asked him, saying, What shall we do then? He
answereth and saith unto them, He that hath two coats, let
him impart to him that hath none; and he that hath meat,
let him do likewise. Then came also publicans to be baptized, and said unto him, Master, what shall we do? And he
said unto them, Exact no more than that which is appointed
you. And the soldiers likewise demanded of him, saying,
And what shall we do? And he said unto them, Do violence
to no man, neither accuse any falsely; and be content with
your wages. And as the people were in expectation, and all
men mused in their hearts of John, whether he were the
Christ, or not; John answered, saying unto them all, I indeed
baptize you with water; but one mightier than I cometh, the
latchet of whose shoes I am not worthy to unloose: he shall
baptize you with the Holy Ghost and with fire: whose fan is
in his hand, and he will throughly purge his floor, and will
gather the wheat into his garner; but the chaff he will burn
with fire unquenchable. And many other things in his exhortation preached he unto the people. But Herod the tetrarch,
being reproved by him for Herodias his brother Philip's wife,
and for all the evils which Herod had done, added yet this
above all, that he shut up John in prison.* (Luke 3:1–20)

Knowing that justification is God's way of righteously
dealing with our sin, you can see why John the Baptist's message of repentance was so important.

Some, in seeking to bring the concept of justification to an understandable level have defined justification as, "Just as if I had never sinned." Even though this definition explains the meaning, it overlooks a very important thought. I am so very thankful that my sins have been forgiven, never to be brought up to me again, and I don't want to ever forget the wretchedness of my selfishness and sin in light of what God has done for me. Paul, in Romans 4:7–8, quotes David from Psalm 32:1–2, "Blessed are they whose iniquities are forgiven, and whose sins are covered. Blessed is the man to whom the Lord will not impute sin." In other words, what a joy it is to those who know that their sin is totally put out of sight, whose sinful record has been cleared of all guilt and Christ's righteousness has been put in its place. Take a moment and think about when this happened to you.

Paul spent a good deal of time dealing with the delicate issue of circumcision. He explained that it was not a work to gain acceptance by God, but a mark of identification for those who by faith trusted in God and desired an intimate relationship with Him. Abraham did nothing to earn right-eousness before God or friendship with God. He simply be-lieved. "He staggered not." He did not doubt. He was strong in faith. He was fully persuaded that what God had promised, He was able to perform. He believed that God could and would do the impossible by giving him (at age one hundred) and his ninety-year-old wife a child. (Can you imagine the looks they must have gotten as they walked through the market place when Sarah was about eight-and-a-half months in her pregnancy?) Romans 4:20–25 is full of faith-packed words.

> [Abraham] *staggered not at the promise of God through unbelief; but was strong in faith, giving glory to God; and being fully persuaded that, what he had promised, he was able also to perform. And therefore it was imputed to him for righteousness. Now it was not written for his sake alone, that it was imputed to him; but for us also, to whom it shall*

*be imputed, if we believe on him that raised up Jesus our
Lord from the dead; who was delivered for our offences, and
was raised again for our justification.* (Romans 4:20–25)

*Therefore it is of faith, that it might be by grace (Romans
4:16a).*

I must trust in the grace of God. Grace is a gift and therefore unmerited, undeserved, and unable to be earned. You
can't buy it, earn it, steal it, or trade for it. It is a gift. A gift is
not a gift if has to be paid for or earned.

*For the wages of sin is death; but the gift of God is eternal
life through Jesus Christ our Lord.* (Romans 6:23)

Romans 6:23 mentions both something earned and
something given. What is the wage (earnings) of sin? Death.
You have to work to earn death. What is the gift of God
through Jesus Christ? Eternal life! This is a free gift from
God. Now, just as grace and eternal life are gifts from God,
men have to *work* to receive God's wrath and judgment. They
earn God's wrath by rejecting Him and despising (treating as
worthless) the riches of His goodness (His grace) with their
hard and impenitent hearts (Romans 2:4–5). It really does
not make sense. Why would anyone choose to earn God's
wrath rather than accept His free gift of salvation?

So, justification, which is all wrapped up in forgiveness
and salvation, is the only answer for the sinful misery we
studied in Romans 1–3. Man ruined his life in sin, but God's
remedy is Jesus Christ who gave His all that we may receive
His all. Christ's righteousness was imputed to us. God sees
Christ's righteousness credited to our account. Have you been
justified? What does justification now mean to you?

CHAPTER 8

Justification Experienced

ROMANS 5

jus·ti·fy (jŭs' tə fī), v.

1. To demonstrate or prove to be just, right, or valid.
2. To declare free of blame; absolve.
3. To free (a human) of the guilt and penalty attached to grievous sin.[1]

In Christian theology, justification is God's act of reckoning a sinner righteous before God by the imputation of Christ's righteousness.

Have you ever received a huge care package full of all kinds of gifts? Once you open the bigger box, it is almost like a birthday and Christmas all rolled into one. One by one, you open smaller wrapped packages and don't stop until you have searched the big box to make sure that you did not miss any. As we unpack Romans 5 (God's care package to us), we will see that it is full of many gifts equally as comforting and amazing as God's huge gift of justification. I wish we had the time in this book to study the intricacies of each gift, but we will only be able to take a quick look of each item in God's care package—we have a lifetime to study each facet of each precious gift. Let's get unpacking.

Therefore being justified by faith, we have PEACE

Therefore being justified by faith, we have peace with God through our Lord Jesus Christ. (Romans 5:1)

The word *peace* (*eirene*) occurs ninety-two times in the New Testament, ten of which appear in the book of Romans. Based on a sense of God's favor, it is the serene tranquility and eager acceptance of every situation (good or bad) and every person (pleasant or prickly) that God allows in your life. I cannot think about God's peace without thinking about Paul's comforting words to both the Philippians and the Colossians.

And the peace of God, which passeth all understanding, shall keep your hearts and minds through Christ Jesus. (Philippians 4:7)

And let the peace of God rule in your hearts, to the which also ye are called in one body; and be ye thankful. (Colossians 3:15)

Sometimes the true emotion of such a Bible concept is captured in song. Many songs that emphasize the peace of God have been written over the years. One that has always struck a chord of real peace in my own heart was written by W. D. Cornell, who captured the essence of "Wonderful Peace" in his hymn.

Far away in the depths of my spirit tonight
Rolls a melody sweeter than psalm;
In celestial-like strains it unceasingly falls
Over my soul like an infinite calm.
Peace, peace, wonderful peace,
Coming down from the Father above;
Sweep over my spirit forever, I pray,
In fathomless billows of love!

What a treasure I have in this wonderful peace,
Buried deep in the heart of my soul,
So secure that no power can mine it away,

While the years of eternity roll!
Peace, peace, wonderful peace,
Coming down from the Father above;
Sweep over my spirit forever, I pray,
In fathomless billows of love!

I am resting tonight in this wonderful peace,
Resting sweetly in Jesus' control;
For I'm kept from all danger by night and by day,
And His glory is flooding my soul!
Peace, peace, wonderful peace,
Coming down from the Father above;
Sweep over my spirit forever, I pray,
In fathomless billows of love!

And I think when I rise to that city of peace,
Where the Author of peace I shall see,
That one strain of the song which the ransomed will sing
In that heavenly kingdom will be:
Peace, peace, wonderful peace,
Coming down from the Father above;
Sweep over my spirit forever, I pray,
In fathomless billows of love!

Ah, soul, are you here without comfort and rest,
Marching down the rough pathway of time?
Make Jesus your Friend ere the shadows grow dark;
O accept of this peace so sublime!
Peace, peace, wonderful peace,
Coming down from the Father above;
Sweep over my spirit forever, I pray,
In fathomless billows of love!

—*W. D. Cornell, 1889*

Therefore being justified by faith, we have GRACE

By whom also we have access by faith into this grace
wherein we stand, and rejoice in hope of the glory of God.
(Romans 5:2)

The word grace (*charis*) is almost too big to wrap your mind around. It is a divine enablement freely given as an expression of God's love and kindness to us. When it is at work, this grace enables, empowers, and encourages us to say "no" to sin and "yes" to God. Grace saves, not just from the past penalty of sin, but from the present power of sin. When we accept God's grace, we will experience both the power and the desire to please Him. If someone asks you how the grace of God impacts your life, you would have to use Philippians 2:13, Hebrews 12:15, and 1 Peter 5:5–11 to answer the question. God freely gives His grace, but we too often fail to accept it. A humble heart looks for grace while a proud heart doesn't think it needs it. If we are blind to our selfish pride, we are in danger of living outside the divine enabling effect of God's grace.

For it is God which worketh in you both to will and to do of
his good pleasure. (Philippians 2:13)

Looking diligently lest any man fail of the grace of God; lest
any root of bitterness springing up trouble you, and thereby
many be defiled. (Hebrews 12:15)

Likewise, ye younger, submit yourselves unto the elder. Yea,
all of you be subject one to another, and be clothed with
humility: for God resisteth the proud, and giveth grace to the
humble. Humble yourselves therefore under the mighty hand
of God, that he may exalt you in due time: casting all your
care upon him; for he careth for you. Be sober, be vigilant;
because your adversary the devil, as a roaring lion, walketh
about, seeking whom he may devour: whom resist stedfast in
the faith, knowing that the same afflictions are accomplished
in your brethren that are in the world. But the God of all
grace, who hath called us unto his eternal glory by Christ
Jesus, after that ye have suffered a while, make you perfect,

*stablish, strengthen, settle you. To him be glory and domin-
ion for ever and ever. Amen.* (1 Peter 5:5–11)

Again, God's concept of grace has found its way into our
hearts through hymns and songs for many years. God's grace
certainly is amazing, and was amazing even before the song
"Amazing Grace" was ever penned. Another great hymn to
meditate on is titled "Marvelous Grace." Slowly read (or even
sing) this classic to yourself and remind yourself that God's
marvelous grace is greater than all your sin.

Marvelous grace of our loving Lord,
Grace that exceeds our sin and our guilt,
Yonder on Calvary's mount outpoured,
There where the blood of the Lamb was spilt.

Grace, grace, God's grace,
Grace that will pardon and cleanse within;
Grace, grace, God's grace,
Grace that is greater than all our sin.

Sin and despair like the sea waves cold
Threaten the soul with infinite loss;
Grace that is greater, yes, grace untold,
Points to the Refuge, the mighty Cross.

Grace, grace, God's grace,
Grace that will pardon and cleanse within;
Grace, grace, God's grace,
Grace that is greater than all our sin.

Marvelous, infinite, matchless grace,
Freely bestowed on all who believe;
You that are longing to see His face,
Will you this moment His grace receive?

Grace, grace, God's grace,
Grace that will pardon and cleanse within;
Grace, grace, God's grace,
Grace that is greater than all our sin.

—Julia H. Johnston, 1911

Therefore being justified by faith, we have HOPE

By whom also we have access by faith into this grace
wherein we stand, and rejoice in hope of the glory of God.
And not only so, but we glory in tribulations also: knowing
that tribulation worketh patience; and patience, experi-
ence; and experience, hope: and hope maketh not ashamed;
because the love of God is shed abroad in our hearts by the
Holy Ghost which is given unto us. (Romans 5:2–5)

I hope you can understand what hope is all about. Hope (*elpis*) is a confident expectation and a joyful anticipation of God's goodness. It may be the joyful anticipation of eternal life in heaven with all its wonders, joys, and opportunities to thank God for what He has done for us. Or it might be the confident expectation that God is going to bring good out of a very difficult situation in life. Earlier in this section, we read about Abraham's justification from Romans 4:18–21. What did Abraham's hope rest in? What does your hope rest in? Read what Edward Mote so clearly penned in his song entitled, "The Solid Rock."

My hope is built on nothing less
Than Jesus' blood and righteousness.
I dare not trust the sweetest frame,
But wholly trust in Jesus' name.

On Christ the solid rock I stand,
All other ground is sinking sand;
All other ground is sinking sand.

—Edward Mote, circa 1834

Therefore being justified by faith, we have the
HOLY SPIRIT

And hope maketh not ashamed; because the love of God is shed abroad in our hearts by the Holy Ghost which is given unto us. (Romans 5:5)

God's Spirit dwells in our spiritual hearts by faith for the purpose of comforting and convicting us. No man has ever seen God the Father! We learn in the first chapter of Colossians that Jesus Christ is the visible icon of the invisible God. If you want to see God the Father or understand the way the Holy Spirit of God works, study the life of Jesus Christ. In Jesus Christ the fullness of Deity (all of it) dwells in His bodily form. When Jesus ascended up into heaven to be with His heavenly Father, He sent His Holy Spirit back to dwell in the hearts of all believers. Being filled with the Holy Spirit means to be totally controlled by Him. This is a choice. We choose whether we are controlled by our selfish flesh or by God's Holy Spirit. How do you know who or what is in control? Check out the checklists in Galatians 5. One lists the characteristics of being controlled by the desires (lusts) of the flesh, and the other describes what will be seen in our lives when we are controlled by God's Spirit. It is a no-brainer choosing which list of characteristics we should desire in our lives. Who would rather lust than love? Who desires hatred, envy, and strife over peace? We always want the positive consequences, but we are not always willing to be controlled by God's Spirit over our own selfish flesh.

Lust of the Flesh	Fruit of the Spirit
Adultery	Love
Fornication	Joy
Uncleanness	Peace
Lasciviousness	Longsuffering
Idolatry	Gentleness
Witchcraft	Goodness

Lust of the Flesh	Fruit of the Spirit
Hatred	Faithfulness
Variance	Meekness
Emulations	Temperance
Wrath	
Strife	
Seditions	
Heresies	
Envyings	
Murders	
Drunkenness	
Revellings	

Therefore being justified by faith, we have the
LOVE OF GOD

*And hope maketh not ashamed; because the love of God is
shed abroad in our hearts by the Holy Ghost which is given
unto us. For when we were yet without strength, in due time
Christ died for the ungodly. For scarcely for a righteous man
will one die: yet peradventure for a good man some would
even dare to die. But God commendeth His love toward us,
in that, while we were yet sinners, Christ died for us. Much
more then, being now justified by His blood, we shall be
saved from wrath through Him.* (Romans 5:5–9)

Love (*agape*) is often misunderstood. God's love is an
undeserved, willing, affectionate care for us. God gives—not
always what we want but always what we need. You have to
love the literal meaning of the words *shed abroad*. This phrase
literally means to be "poured out" and was used in the sacrificial system for the atonement of sin. Romans 5:6–9 describes
the love that God poured out for us in the pouring out of
Jesus' blood by which we sinners were justified. Got all that?
How long has it been since you personally thanked God for
loving you and saving you? I love the first and the last verses
of Frederick Lehman's hymn classic "The Love of God."

*The love of God is greater far than tongue or pen can
     ever tell;*
*It goes beyond the highest star and reaches to the lowest
     hell;*
*The guilty pair, bowed down with care, God gave His Son
     to win;*
His erring child He reconciled and pardoned from his sin.
Oh, love of God, how rich and pure!
How measureless and strong!
It shall forevermore endure—
the saints' and angels' song.

*Could we with ink the ocean fill, and were the skies of
     parchment made,*
*Were every stalk on earth a quill, and every man a scribe
     by trade;*
To write the love of God above would drain the ocean dry;
*Nor could the scroll contain the whole, though stretched
     from sky to sky.*
Oh, love of God, how rich and pure!
How measureless and strong!
It shall forevermore endure—
the saints' and angels' song.

—Frederick Lehman, 1917

Therefore being justified by faith, we have been RECONCILED TO GOD

*For if, when we were enemies, we were reconciled to God by
the death of his Son, much more, being reconciled, we shall
be saved by his life.* (Romans 5:10)

The word *reconcile* (*katallasso*) conveys the idea of restoring a broken relationship to a healthy relationship. Because of our sin, we were considered enemies of God. Now, because of our reconciliation and justification, we are considered friends of God. How many of your friends know for sure that you are a "friend of God"? How would they know that?

There is not a better passage of Scripture that deals with the blessing of our reconciliation to God and our ministry of reconciling others to God than 2 Corinthians 5:17–21. To paraphrase, Paul basically is telling us that once we are in Christ, we are a new creation. The old is passed away and is being replaced with the new. This is from God, Who through Christ, reconciled us to Himself and then gave to us the ministry of reconciliation by trusting us with the message of reconciliation. Now we are ambassadors for Christ and God makes His appeal through us. We beg, plead, and implore those who do not know Christ to be reconciled to God through Christ. For us, God made Christ to be sin (Who never sinned and knew no sin), so that in Christ's righteousness we might become righteous in the sight of God. Isn't our Lord wonderful?

Therefore being justified by faith, we are no longer viewed as *sinners* because of one man's disobedience (Adam's), but are viewed as *righteous* because of one Man's obedience (Jesus Christ's), as taught in Romans 5:12–21.

When you put your faith in Jesus Christ and trusted Him and Him alone for the forgiveness of your sins, God no longer looked at you as a sinner outside of Christ but as a righteous person because of Christ. Think about the gifts God listed for us in Romans 5. The righteous, who have been justified by faith, have received the gifts of peace, grace, hope, God's Holy Spirit, God's love, and the privilege of being reconciled to God Himself! That is a care package like no other. Now, those who reject God's goodness and look down on His grace will receive tribulation, anguish, indignation, and God's wrath as their earned, eternal wages. Take a minute to thank God for what He has given you. Thank God for your spiritual care package. Again, what a wonderful God we have!

CHAPTER 9

Sanctification: Our Position in Christ

ROMANS 6

Go to the Kentucky Derby and watch the jockeys maneuver for a better position. Visit a NASCAR race and hope that your favorite driver has earned the pole position (the starting position inside of the front row). As a sinner, when I put my faith and trust in Jesus Christ's redemptive work, my position changed—for the better. *Positionally*, I was dead in sin; now I am alive to God! *Positionally*, I was a defeated slave to sin; now I am a victorious servant of God. When God saved me and positioned me "in Christ" that was the beginning of His progressive sanctification process in my life. God is so good.

Romans 6:1–11 explains that we are to consider ourselves "in Christ" both in His death and in His resurrection. Being positioned "in Christ" means that we are to be dead to the power of sin and alive to God! The entire chapter of Romans 6 can be divided into two simple thoughts seen in Romans 6:11 and Romans 6:12.

The first half of Romans 6 (eleven verses) deals with the past and is explained in Romans 6:11: "Likewise reckon ye also yourselves to be dead indeed unto sin, but alive unto God through Jesus Christ our Lord."

The second half of Romans 6 (twelve verses) deals with our future and clearly commands in Romans 6:12: "Let not sin therefore reign in your mortal body, that ye should obey it in the lusts thereof."

Romans 6:11 condenses the first eleven verses: "Likewise reckon ye also yourselves to be dead indeed unto sin, but alive unto God through Jesus Christ our Lord." Consider yourself dead to sin. You don't have to sin anymore. Sin is not the boss of you, and you can say "No!" Unless you live in the hills of the Great Smoky Mountains, you probably have not used the phrase, "I reckon." To "reckon" is to consider, imagine, or think. God's sanctification process involves thinking—thinking clearly and thinking biblically.

The constant battles fought in our selfish, lazy, corrupt minds are humiliating, discouraging, and would be incredibly embarrassing if anyone knew what really went on in the midst of all that gray matter. God wants us to think. God wants us to think in a way that pleases Him, which will demand the "renewing" of our minds. The renewing of the mind is part of the biblical change process as seen in Ephesians 4:22–24.

Put off → Renew the mind → Put on

That ye put off concerning the former conversation the old man, which is corrupt according to the deceitful lusts; and be renewed in the spirit of your mind; and that ye put on the new man, which after God is created in righteousness and true holiness. (Ephesians 4:22–24)

Renewing the mind takes time—day-by-day kind of time.

For which cause we faint not; but though our outward man perish, yet the inward man is renewed day by day. (2 Corinthians 4:16)

The renewing of the mind is a foundation for transformation into Christlikeness.

And be not conformed to this world: but be ye transformed by the renewing of your mind, that ye may prove what is that good, and acceptable, and perfect, will of God. (Romans 12:2)

The renewing of the mind is essential for biblical change. Romans 6:11 shows us how to think and what to think. Our old flesh (the sinful nature) usually disagrees. Reckon, think, consider yourself dead to what? Reckon, think, and consider yourself alive to whom?

Paul illustrated this aspect of our sanctification with baptism.

> *Know ye not, that so many of us as were baptized into Jesus Christ were baptized into his death? Therefore we are buried with him by baptism into death: that like as Christ was raised up from the dead by the glory of the Father, even so we also should walk in newness of life. For if we have been planted together in the likeness of his death, we shall be also in the likeness of his resurrection: knowing this, that our old man is crucified with him, that the body of sin might be de stroyed, that henceforth we should not serve sin.* (Romans 6:3–6)

These young Roman Christians already knew that water baptism was a public display of their personal identification with Jesus' death, burial, and resurrection, testifying that they were totally immersed in Jesus Christ. If someone did not attend your baptismal service, how would they know that you are positioned, identified, and immersed "in Christ" today?

The answer to this question is found in our second half of this chapter, which is summed up in these words:

> *"Let not sin therefore reign in your mortal body, that ye should obey it in the lusts thereof."* (Romans 6:12)

Both believers and unbelievers can observe what you are on the inside (the real you) by watching what or whom you submit yourself to as the king of your life! If one of your family members was asked who or what is the king in your life, what would they say? There are six reasons in the last eleven verses of Romans 6 that tell us why we should submit to God as King instead of being enslaved to sin as master.

Why submit to God as King?

• Because God has brought you from death to life!

Neither yield ye your members as instruments of unright-
eousness unto sin: but yield yourselves unto God, as those
that are alive from the dead, and your members as instru-
ments of righteousness unto God. (Romans 6:13)

At salvation, you were united with Christ in His death, burial, and resurrection. You were in line to receive sin's wage (eternal death), but you chose to step out of line, turn to Christ, and receive God's gift (eternal life).

Why submit to God as King?

- Because you are under grace!

For sin shall not have dominion over you: for ye are not
under the law, but under grace. (Romans 6:14)

Grace dethrones sin as lord and replaces it with the Lord Jesus Christ. God's grace is the divine enablement to say "no" to the reign of sin. When Paul wrote to Titus, he reminded him that grace teaches us to "deny ungodliness and worldly lusts, we should live soberly, righteously, and godly, in this present world" (Titus 2:12).

Why submit to God as King?

- Because of the principle of bondage!

Know ye not, that to whom ye yield yourselves servants to
obey, his servants ye are to whom ye obey; whether of sin unto
death, or of obedience unto righteousness? (Romans 6:16)

Paul is trying to bring his readers back to their senses: "Don't you know, don't you understand, don't you realize that you will become the slave of whomever or whatever you choose to obey?" If sin is your master and lord, what do you have to look forward to in this life? If God is your Master and Lord what do you have to look forward to in this life and all eternity?

Why submit to God as King?

- Because this is a heart issue, and it is in your heart to do so!

But God be thanked, that ye were the servants of sin, but ye
have obeyed from the heart that form of doctrine which was

delivered you. Being then made free from sin, ye became the
servants of righteousness. (Romans 6:17–18)

Paul thanked God that these Roman Christians obeyed
from the heart! This is huge! We can obey from fear of what
others will think about us, or we can obey from the heart
because we simply love God. Do you obey God out of duty or
devotion? Do you find yourself wanting to stay pure, control your tongue, and serve others because you "want to" or
because you "have to"? God is so pleased with a heart that
believes and obeys.

Why submit to God as King?

- Because consequences are a result of life's choices!

  What fruit had ye then in those things whereof ye are now
  ashamed? For the end of those things is death. But now
  being made free from sin, and become servants to God, ye
  have your fruit unto holiness, and the end everlasting life.
  For the wages of sin is death; but the gift of God is eternal
  life through Jesus Christ our Lord. (Romans 6:21–23)

I trust that you have personally chosen God's free gift of
salvation. One of the surest signs of salvation, characteristics
of a Christian, or spiritual birthmarks of a believer is the obvious progress in your sanctification. When you are fruitful
in this life, you need not be fearful about eternal life.

CHAPTER 10

Sanctification: Our Problem with Sin

ROMANS 7

A quick read of Romans 7 should both humble us and remind us that we are totally incapable of ever doing anything good. I have a friend who was raised in a denomination that taught that you had to earn your own salvation and do good things to gain God's favor. He tried. In fact, he tried hard by going to church, reciting religious phrases, and faithfully confessing his sins at confession. As a teen, he knew he could not be "good enough" to keep all the rules and regulations, so he gave up. He knew that he could not keep all the "laws of the church," and he assumed that he was destined to hell. In his early twenties, he heard the true gospel for the first time and accepted Christ as his Savior. He actually lived Romans 7–8 without even knowing that it was in the Bible. With these thoughts in mind, slowly read through the following portion of Romans 7.

> *What shall we say then? Is the law sin? God forbid. Nay, I had not known sin, but by the law: for I had not known lust, except the law had said, Thou shalt not covet. But sin, taking occasion by the commandment, wrought in me all manner of concupiscence. For without the law sin was dead. For I*

*was alive without the law once: but when the command-
ment came, sin revived, and I died. And the commandment,
which was ordained to life, I found to be unto death. For sin,
taking occasion by the commandment, deceived me, and by
it slew me. Wherefore the law is holy, and the commandment holy, and just, and good. Was then that which is good
made death unto me? God forbid. But sin, that it might
appear sin, working death in me by that which is good; that
sin by the commandment might become exceeding sinful.
For we know that the law is spiritual: but I am carnal, sold
under sin. For that which I do I allow not: for what I would,
that do I not; but what I hate, that do I. If then I do that
which I would not, I consent unto the law that it is good.
Now then it is no more I that do it, but sin that dwelleth in
me. For I know that in me (that is, in my flesh,) dwelleth no
good thing: for to will is present with me; but how to perform that which is good I find not. For the good that I would
I do not: but the evil which I would not, that I do. Now if I
do that I would not, it is no more I that do it, but sin that
dwelleth in me. I find then a law, that, when I would do
good, evil is present with me. For I delight in the law of God
after the inward man: but I see another law in my members, warring against the law of my mind, and bringing me
into captivity to the law of sin which is in my members. O
wretched man that I am! Who shall deliver me from the
body of this death? I thank God through Jesus Christ our
Lord. So then with the mind I myself serve the law of God;
but with the flesh the law of sin.* (Romans 7:7–25)

We Christians have a problem dealing with our sinful
flesh. It could seem hopeless. What do you do on a daily basis
to control your flesh? What do you do to change your flesh?
What do you do to conquer the flesh? How did Paul and his
ministry friends deal with the flesh?

Paul came to a realization that every one of us needs to
understand and admit. Hear the emotion in his statement,
"O wretched man that I am! Who shall deliver me from
this body of death?" We are so wicked and so weak that
it would be hopeless if we had to deal with our sin in our

own strength. We need Romans 8! I can't be good enough (as explained in Romans 7), and I must depend on Christ and Christ alone to deliver me (as explained in Romans 8). Romans 7 helps us to concentrate on our needs, our unworthiness, our sinfulness, our wickedness, and our inability to ever do anything good in ourselves.

Pretend you are dead (Romans 7:1–6)

Five times in the first six verses of Romans 7 Paul uses the word *dead* to illustrate and explain how we should view our relationship with the law (doing good things to gain a good standing). Possums play dead. If a grizzly bear is attacking you, you had better play dead. To play dead you need to think dead and act dead. Dead people cannot talk, see, or think. They are dead! Can a dead person ride a bike? Why not? Can a dead person answer his cell phone? Why not? Can a dead person keep the law and do good?

See how terrible your sin really is (Romans 7:7–13)

God's law is not sinful, it simply shows me how sinful I am. Salvation is not a choice between heaven and hell, but between Jesus Christ and my sin. It is my sin that enslaves; it is my sin that controls; it is my sin that separates me from God. The more I understand God's Word the more I am aware of my incredibly wicked heart; the more I understand my sinful heart, the more thankful I am for what God has done for me. God's commandments are holy, just, and good. They reveal what I am, what I need, and how Christ can meet that need. It is holy, just, and good to honor your parents. It is holy, just, and good to not kill, commit adultery, or to steal. The commandments of God are all holy, just, and good both for us and those we would have chosen to sin against.

If we did not have God's written laws, commandments, precepts, testimonies, statutes, and righteous judgments, we would not know that we were wretched sinners in need of a wonderful Savior. Do you view your sin in the same way that God views your sin? It would benefit us all to often pray through David's prayer from Psalm 139:23–24, asking God to reveal to us any unknown sin that may be hiding in our hearts.

> *Search me, O God, and know my heart: try me, and know my thoughts: and see if there be any wicked way in me, and lead me in the way everlasting.* (Psalm 139:23–24)

What a battle! Will it ever end? (Romans 7:14–25)

Have you ever thought something like this, "I don't get it! The things I hate to do, I do, and the things I should do, I don't do!" If so, join the club. Don't fret. Paul is part of our club too. The more you mature in Christ, the more you hate your sin. The more you grow in your sanctification process, the greater will be your abhorrence of the sin that holds you back from Christlikeness. Is there anything that you know you should do, but you struggle in both the consistency and commitment to do it? Are there any evil things that you consistently do, but wish you could stop? If you had to say "yes" to either or both of those questions, you may want to cry out with Paul, "O wretched man that I am! Who shall deliver me from the body of this death? I thank God through Jesus Christ our Lord."

CHAPTER 11

Sanctification: Our Power in Christ

ROMANS 8

We need Romans 8! We can't be good enough (as explained in Romans 7), and we must depend on Christ and Christ alone to deliver us (as explained in Romans 8). All Scripture is inspired by God. Some verses, because of their directness and clarity, seem to easily grab hold of our attention and are often memorized and chosen as favorites. Romans 8 has at least ten such verses. An understanding of each of these classic passages will encourage our hearts to love our God even more.

There is therefore now no condemnation to them which are in Christ Jesus, who walk not after the flesh, but after the Spirit. (Romans 8:1)

For those of us who belong to Christ Jesus, who by faith have recognized our guilt before God and trusted in God's grace, who have accepted His forgiveness through Christ's death on the cross, who are not trusting in any good that we have done, who are relying only on what Christ has done for us, there is not one hint of condemnation. None! There is no condemning judgment against us. We have been forgiven and freed from the penalty of all our sin. God's forgiveness is a promise, and He will never again rebuke us, criticize us, reprimand us, blame us, reprove us, or hold us accountable for that sin. Amen.

> *For ye have not received the spirit of bondage again to fear; but ye have received the Spirit of adoption, whereby we cry, Abba, Father. The Spirit itself beareth witness with our spirit, that we are the children of God: and if children, then heirs; heirs of God, and joint-heirs with Christ; if so be that we suffer with him, that we may be also glorified together.* (Romans 8:15–17)

I have a special relationship with God. It is not the relationship of a fearful slave but of a forgiven son. God adopted me! He chose me even though I did not deserve it. He is a loving Father Whom I can trust, depend on, and love with all my heart. This relationship involves His Spirit dwelling in me, affirming and assuring me that I am His child and that someday (I can't wait) I will be in His presence sharing in all His glory. The difficult times of suffering because I am identified with Christ do not even compare with what God has for me in heaven some day. "Thank you, my wonderful God and loving Father."

> *Likewise the Spirit also helpeth our infirmities: for we know not what we should pray for as we ought: but the Spirit itself maketh intercession for us with groanings which cannot be uttered.* (Romans 8:26)

When I get so overwhelmed with my obvious weaknesses, infirmities, and helplessness, God's indwelling Spirit is there to help me, strengthen me, and even pray for me. There are times I just shake my head because I don't know what to do or say. I can't even pray! That's when the Holy Spirit intervenes and intercedes for me by expressing my crushed heart's anguish with groanings so deep that they cannot be expressed in words. What a wonderful God we have! Have you ever approached God in prayer, not even knowing what to pray, and just fallen before Him? If so, then you understand Romans 8:26.

And we know that all things work together for good to them that love God, to them who are the called according to his purpose. For whom he did foreknow, he also did predestinate to be conformed to the image of his Son, that he might be the firstborn among many brethren. (Romans 8:28–29)

All things—good or bad. All things—beneficial or difficult. All things—pleasurable or painful. Everything that happens in my life is designed to help me become more like Jesus Christ. This is God's good goal for me; this is God's purpose for my life; and all I need to do is to love my God more and more each day. I know I am called. I know my God is in control. I know that God has had a plan for my life for a long time. "Lord, help me to love you with my whole heart, soul, mind, and strength."

Nay, in all these things we are more than conquerors through him that loved us. (Romans 8:37)

Just because we have trouble and hard times or experience hunger, poverty, or even death threats, does not mean that God does not love us. Despite all these things, we will be eternally victorious because of God's love to us. We won't be just conquerors, but more than conquerors. If God is for us, who can be against us? If God is for us, who can accuse us? God is for us. God loves us. Amazing.

For I am persuaded, that neither death, nor life, nor angels, nor principalities, nor powers, nor things present, nor things to come, nor height, nor depth, nor any other creature, shall be able to separate us from the love of God, which is in Christ Jesus our Lord. (Romans 8:38–39)

I am convinced, I am persuaded, I am assured that nothing, absolutely nothing . . .

- neither death or life,
- neither angels or demons,
- neither present worries or future fears,
- neither anything from the sky above or the earth below, nothing in all of God's creation . . . including my own selfish heart,

- nothing, *absolutely nothing,*

. . . can separate me from God's love that He revealed to me through the life, death, burial, and resurrection of His Son, Jesus Christ.

CHAPTER 12

Sovereignty: God Is in Control

ROMANS 9-11

I wish we had the time and the room in this study to dig deeper into Israel's past election, present rejection, and future redemption as taught in Romans 9–11. Although there are teachings in this passage that are difficult to grasp and hard to understand, we must recognize that God has some mysteries and secrets that He is certainly entitled to. If I could totally understand the dynamic tension between God's sovereignty and man's free will, I would be God. I am not God and am more than willing to trust Him as a fair, just, loving, kind, and sovereign God. I think this is why God inspired Paul to end this second section of Romans in this way.

> O the depth of the riches both of the wisdom and knowledge of God! How unsearchable are his judgments, and his ways past finding out! For who hath known the mind of the Lord? Or who hath been his counselor? Or who hath first given to him, and it shall be recompensed unto him again? For of him, and through him, and to him, are all things: to whom be glory for ever. Amen. (Romans 11:33–36)

What can we learn from Israel's past election by God (Romans 9:1–33)? I really cannot summarize the truths of

Romans 9 any better than commentator Warren Wiersbe has in his *Expository Outlines on the New Testament*: "Paul's purpose in this chapter is to explain Israel's position in the plan of God. Israel was an elect nation, given privileges that no other nation had; yet it failed miserably to follow God's program of blessing for the world. The entire chapter exalts the sovereign grace of God without minimizing the responsibility of men and women for making right decisions. God's Word will prevail regardless of human disobedience; but disobedient sinners will miss the blessing."[1]

You can't read through Romans 9 without realizing that we have a wonderful and powerfully sovereign God Who is in control. It is hard to understand why anyone would want to reject God's offer of redemption. Although God's election is difficult to grasp in our finite minds, we do know that according to Romans 9:14, we are never to accuse God of being unrighteous or unfair. No man, woman, or teen "deserves" to be forgiven and saved from his or her sin. If you have experienced God's forgiveness, it should humble you until all you can say to God is, "Thank You, thank You, thank You." Maybe it would be good to stop reading for a few minutes and write a sincere thank-you note to God expressing your gratitude for the free gift of salvation that you have received.

What can we learn from Israel's present rejection of God (Romans 10:1–21)? Paul loved his people and wanted them to have a right relationship with God—God's way. God's way is simple; God's way must be shared with sinners; God's way is the only way—but it is available for all who will believe. Are there any more comforting and all inclusive words than these?

> *That if thou shalt confess with thy mouth the Lord Jesus, and shalt believe in thine heart that God hath raised him from the dead, thou shalt be saved. For with the heart man believeth unto righteousness; and with the mouth confession is made unto salvation.* (Romans 10:9–10)

> *For whosoever shall call upon the name of the Lord shall be saved.* (Romans 10:13)

If you want to call Bible Christianity a religion, there are only two religions in the entire world. Getting right with God through *works* is one and getting right with God through *faith* is the other. No one will ever get to God by being good enough—it will never happen. Everyone can get to God by trusting Jesus Christ, Who can and will forgive all sins for those who believe. As a whole, the nation of Israel rejected God's way and therefore rejected eternity with God. Do you know anyone who has made the same choice? Doesn't your heart break for them?

What can we learn from Israel's future redemption by God, taught in Romans 11:1–36? We can learn that God is a merciful God. He wants Israel as a whole to repent and believe the gospel. He is both kind and severe in His treatment of those who hear the truth of the gospel—kind to those who believe the truth and severe to those who reject it. His mercy is available for all (Jew or Gentile) who will believe. God has a plan and no matter who rejects His plan or seeks to change it, He will accomplish it in His sovereignty and timing. This should make us sing with Paul:

> *O the depth of the riches both of the wisdom and knowledge of God! How unsearchable are his judgments, and his ways past finding out! For who hath known the mind of the Lord? Or who hath been his counselor? Or who hath first given to him, and it shall be recompensed unto him again? For of him, and through him, and to him, are all things: to whom be glory for ever. Amen.* (Romans 11:33–36)

SECTION 3

Twenty-Four Ways I Can Show My Thankfulness for God's Deliverance

ROMANS 12

+   +   +

We learned in the first section of our study how depraved and wicked man's heart can become when he refuses to listen to God and pushes Him out of his life. When God is rejected and despised, evil reigns. The solution for such a wicked, depraved, sinful heart is its rescue, redemption, and reconciliation through Jesus Christ.

God's remedy is in Jesus Christ

In our overview of Romans 4–11 in the second section of this study, we learned that God's remedy for man's ruined life in sin is found in the life, death, burial, and resurrection of Jesus Christ. Being justified and sanctified in Christ gives us the special privilege of having our sins forgiven and experiencing a right relationship with the one and only true God.

Therefore, how can I show my thankfulness to God for such a deliverance?

Romans 12–16 is full of practical principles and practices on how a forgiven sinner (now in Christ) should think, act, and live in a world of pride, strife, tension, hypocrisy, rebellion, evil, disobedience, lust, and a myriad of other sinful practices. Too many believers forget what God has done for them and therefore do not feel the compulsion to thank Him on a daily basis. How does a man say "thank you" to a God Who has done so much for him? The answer is in Romans 12. The conclusion of our study will reveal twenty-four ways to say "thank you" to our wonderful God for what He so sacrificially has done for us.

CHAPTER 13

Understand Paul's "Therefore"

Therefore

Paul's "therefores" are always there for a specific reason. Whenever we find the word *therefore* we must look back and see what it is there for. A *therefore* in Scripture is a carabiner of truth often connecting a specific cause with a desired effect. Many commentators use *therefores* to compare the relationship between doctrine and duty, belief and behavior, doctrinal teaching and exhortational preaching.

As mentioned earlier in our study, some Bible scholars have summarized the book of Romans in three simple statements, seeking to answer the question: How many things does a person have to know to live and die a happy, contented, and fulfilled life? Only three!

1. How great are my miseries and sin (Romans 1–3)
2. How I can be delivered from my misery and sin (Romans 4–11)
3. How I am to be thankful to God for such deliverance (Romans 12)

What has God saved you from? Think about the seriousness of your sinful condition before God reconciled you to Himself.

What did God do to save you from your miserable sins, justify you, and put you in a right relationship with Himself?

What should be your spiritual, reasonable, rational, sensible, logical, commonsensical response to God for His forgiveness and redemption?

I am personally being mentored by some men whom God has gifted with incredible understanding of His Word. Although I've never sat down in a coffee shop with any of these guys, they have shared their hearts in print (some written hundreds of years ago) for me to learn from. Hopefully, during the millennial reign, I will be able to thank them personally for what they have done for me (maybe even in a coffee shop over a cinnamon dulce latte). Here is some of the encouragement I've received from my meditating mentors.

Therefore . . . from the viewpoint of Donald Grey Barnhouse:

> The 'therefore' of chapter twelve must look back over the entire epistle and divide its revelation under two heads: (1) man's complete ruin in sin, and, (2) God's perfect remedy in Christ. Sin and salvation—this is the burden and the joy of the gospel, and this is the foundation for the practical, day by day Christian life.[1]

Therefore . . . from the viewpoint of Warren Wiersbe:

> In the Christian life, doctrine and duty always go together. What we believe helps to determine how we behave. It is not enough for us to understand Paul's doctrinal explanations. We must translate our learning into living and show by our daily lives that we trust God's Word. If we have a right relationship to God, we will have a right relationship to the people who are a part of our lives. "If a man say, I love God, and hateth his brother, he is a liar" (1 John 4:20).[2]

Therefore . . . from the viewpoint of William Hendriksen and Simon Kistemaker:

> What the apostle is saying is that in view of God's mercy, a voluntary and enthusiastic response of gratitude is required. What he is saying, then, is that this sovereign divine mercy calls for a life of complete dedication and

wholehearted commitment. Animal sacrifices will not do! Nothing less than thorough self-surrender out of gratitude is required. What the apostle is teaching, therefore, is that Christian ethics is based on Christian doctrine. Returning once more to the opening chapters of Paul's epistle to the Romans and from there quickly reviewing the remainder of this precious writing, one cannot help becoming aware of the fact that in 1:1–3:20 man's sin and misery are described; in 3:21–11:36 the way of deliverance is opened to him; and in 12:1–16:27 the rescued believer is shown how, by a life of gratitude to God and helpfulness toward God's children and, in fact, toward everybody, man should respond.[3]

Therefore . . . from the viewpoint of Joseph Hall:

Doctrine without exhortation makes men all brain, no heart; exhortation without doctrine makes the heart full, but leaves the brain empty. Both together make a man, one makes a wise man, the other a good man; one serves that we may know our duty, the other that we may perform it. Men cannot practice unless they know, and they know in vain if they practice not.[4]

Therefore . . . from the viewpoint of the psalmist David in Psalm 50:15:

[Misery] *Call upon me in the day of trouble;*

[Deliverance] *And I will deliver thee;*

[Gratitude] *And thou shalt glorify me.*

"Thank You, Lord, for showing me my miseries and sin. Thank You, Lord for delivering me from my misery and sin. Therefore, show me how I can daily please You in my relationships with others and with You."

CHAPTER 14

Understand God's Mercies

I beseech you therefore, brethren, by the mercies of God, that ye present your bodies a living sacrifice, holy, acceptable unto God, which is your reasonable service. And be not conformed to this world: but be ye transformed by the renewing of your mind, that ye may prove what is that good, and acceptable, and perfect, will of God. *(Romans 12:1–2)*

I beseech you

What do you do if you beseech someone? Paul is a great beseecher. We don't beseech as much as we should although some beseech and don't even know it. Comparative translations use words such as *plead, urge,* or *appeal.* If you don't understand the full intent of the word, it could come across as a begging of sorts. *The Complete Word Study Dictionary of the New Testament* explains that *beseech* means *to aid, help, comfort,* or *encourage.*[1] *The Exegetical Dictionary of the New Testament* translates *beseech* with the words *request, urge,* and *comfort.*[2] If *beseech* were a fruit, it would be a type of passion fruit growing on a compassion-care tree. The word translated *beseech (parakaleo)* actually comes from two Greek words, one meaning "to call" and the other "along side of." Paul was giving an encouraging, passionate appeal to do what he was already doing. He was basically saying, "Christian brother, come here by my side, and together we will spend our lives thanking God for His unsearchable mercy that we have seen in Jesus Christ, Who paid for both your and my sinful wickedness. God made a way for us to have a right relationship with Him."

The old adage "People don't care how much you know until they know how much you care" fits well with the concept of coming along side of someone to encourage him in his walk with the Lord. Paul was not asking anyone to do anything that he was not already doing himself. He was not harsh or demanding in his request. He did not authoritatively say, "Go sacrifice and do something for God!" He humbly requested, "Come with me, and we will serve our wonderful Lord together." Whether you are a parent, friend, brother, sister, teacher, pastor, counselor, or employer, how do you lead others? (By the way, we are all leaders. By our examples we are either leading others closer to God or farther away from God.)

Brethren

Paul wrote *adelphoi* where we would write *brothers*, *sisters*, or *believing friends*. This is not an evangelistic plea, but a godly man overwhelmed with God's mercies urging his believing friends to give their lives to God. God wants us to reach out to the unsaved as soul-winners, but He also wants us to reach out to wandering believers as soul-rescuers.

Often in the Gospels, Jesus referred to the disciples as brethren. Peter, Stephen, and other preachers in the book of Acts addressed "men and brethren," knowing that all men are not brothers, but all men could be brothers if they trusted in the same heavenly Father. In the thirteen letters (we call them epistles) that Paul wrote to his young, believing friends, Paul referred to brethren over one hundred times—nineteen in the book of Romans alone! Paul wrote letters. We send texts and emails. Paul prayed to discern the specific needs of his brethren and then addressed those issues. Can you think of five Christian brothers or sisters (brethren) who need some encouragement to draw closer to the Lord? What do you do (or should you do) to encourage those five brethren in their walk with God?

By the mercies of God

We all need to be daily reminded of God's mercies. Remember, mercy is keeping from us that which we truly deserve. We deserve to pay the penalty for our own sins, but God, by His mercy, paid it for us. "By the mercies of God" is Paul's credibility clause as he refers to Romans 1–11. God's mercies are almost unbelievable when you realize that these mercies are based on pity, love, and compassion to selfish, unloving, hard-hearted recipients. Paul reminds us in his second letter to the Corinthians in chapter one, verse three that God is not only the God of all comfort but also the Father of all mercies. When you need comfort or compassion, bypass the chain of command, skip the managers, the administrators, the CFO, COO, and CEO—go directly to your loving heavenly Father God!

The opposite of God's mercy is God's wrath. To put a little reverential fear and true thankfulness in our hearts, it is good to paint a picture of these two attributes of God in our minds and compare the implications of each: one deserved—the other undeserved; one petrifying in terms of God's justice—the other overwhelming in terms of God's goodness; one to fear—one to enjoy. Both are of God and both will be seen in their ultimate fashion when God chooses to fulfil the promises of His prophetic Word. Remember . . .

> It is of the Lord's mercies that we are not consumed, because his compassions fail not. They are new every morning: great is thy faithfulness. (Lamentations 3:22–23)

CHAPTER 15

Understand Sacrificial Living

I beseech you therefore, brethren, by the mercies of God, that ye present your bodies a living sacrifice, holy, acceptable unto God, which is your reasonable service. And be not conformed to this world: but be ye transformed by the renewing of your mind, that ye may prove what is that good, and acceptable, and perfect, will of God. *(Romans 12:1–2)*

That ye present your bodies

Paul is encouraging both his friends in Rome and his future friends that he will meet in the Millennium (that's you and me) to present our bodies. How do you do that? Does it mean that you wrap your body up in Christmas wrap and give it as a present? Does it mean that if God calls roll, that you respond with "present"? Do you formally hand your body over to God in a public presentation? What do you think Paul is referring to when he asks those of us who are overwhelmed with God's mercies to present our bodies?

First, according to the *Complete Word Study Dictionary*, *present (paristemi)* comes from two words: *para*, meaning "near," and *histemi,* meaning "to stand near or before"[1]. Secondly, *Thayer's Greek Lexicon* defines the word *present* as meaning "to bring into one's presence," "to stand by," "to be present."[2] Finally, it sometimes helps to understand a principle by examining its opposite. The opposite of *paristemi* is *aphistemi,* which means "to depart or withdraw," "to be absent," "to remove oneself," "to forsake," "to desert."[3] Such desertion is always based on selfishness and pride.

How did James warn those who were living in pride, refusing to resist the Devil, living with filthy hands, impure hearts, and double-minded commitment to God?

> *But He giveth more grace. Wherefore He saith, God resisteth the proud, but giveth grace unto the humble. Submit yourselves therefore to God. Resist the devil, and he will flee from you. Draw nigh to God, and He will draw nigh to you. Cleanse your hands, ye sinners; and purify your hearts, ye double minded. Be afflicted, and mourn, and weep: let your laughter be turned to mourning, and your joy to heaviness. Humble yourselves in the sight of the Lord, and He shall lift you up. (James 4:6–10)*

The word *deserter* carries a picture of a regretful, beaten-down, fearful failure traveling from town to town trying to escape the embarrassing memories of the past and the fear of future humiliation when he is again found out for who he is. We have a choice to make. We can be as close to God as we want to be!

In a way, we should wrap up ourselves as a present to God and when He calls our name, we can immediately say, "Here! Right by your side! Present!" Paul reminds us that this presenting (the willing desire to be close to God) is not just a spiritual thing, but we are to present our physical bodies. Your body is that thing you live in; that thing you have to feed to keep alive; that thing that needs to be clothed to stay warm; that thing that needs sleep and rest at times; that thing that you spend hours painting and working on to look like a good thing before others; that thing that gets you from place to place; that thing that gets you in trouble at times; that thing that is recognized by others; that thing that is made of primarily dust and water and will someday return to such; that thing you call your body! God has much to say about our physical bodies and our relationship with Him.

And the very God of peace sanctify you wholly; and I pray God your whole spirit and soul and body be preserved blameless unto the coming of our Lord Jesus Christ.
(1 Thessalonians 5:23)

Let not sin therefore reign in your mortal body, that ye should obey it in the lusts thereof. (Romans 6:12)

What? Know ye not that your body is the temple of the Holy Ghost which is in you, which ye have of God, and ye are not your own? For ye are bought with a price: therefore glorify God in your body, and in your spirit, which are God's.
(1 Corinthians 6:19–20)

How can you "glorify God in your body"?

- As you say "no" to any temptation that satisfies the lust of the flesh (drugs, alcohol, sex, gluttony, laziness), you magnify God's power over sin.
- As you speak kindly to those who attack you for your relationship with Christ, you magnify God's patience with sinners.
- As you accept difficult physical or financial situations with a calm acceptance, you magnify God's peace in the midst of the storm.
- As you respond in a loving way to very unloving people, you magnify God's persistent love that only He could possibly put in your heart for such people.
- As you hand the "container of your soul" over to God for Him to use any way He so pleases, you magnify God's goodness as you truly believe that He wants the best for your life.

A living sacrifice

What kind of sacrifice is Paul asking us to make? A living sacrifice. A holy sacrifice. An acceptable sacrifice. A sacrifice that pleases God. What is sacrifice? Sacrifice is the willingness to give up something that is very valuable to you, something that you love and cherish very deeply.

Leviticus 1 describes the type of sacrifice that truly pleased God.

- Verse 2—It was sacrificing something needed to sustain life ("of the herd" or "the flock").
- Verse 3—It was sacrificing something very valuable ("without blemish").
- Verse 3—It was sacrificing something that could bring greater wealth or prosperity in the future ("male without blemish" or defect).
- Verse 3—It was a willing, unmanipulated, right-from-the-heart sacrifice ("he shall offer it of his own voluntary will").
- Verses 3 and 5—It was a God-focused sacrifice ("before the Lord").
- Verse 4—It was a personal this-is-for-my-sin sacrifice ("he shall put his hand upon the head of the burnt offering"). (Note: The personal pronouns *he* or *his* are used eleven times.)
- Verse 5—It was a difficult sacrifice: to take the life of that innocent calf or lamb who was dying for me, for my sin, and for no other reason ("he shall kill the bullock"). Verse 5—It was a gruesome and horrific sacrifice, as the method of killing had to be the sticking or cutting of the throat to get the blood for the priests ("the priests . . . shall . . . sprinkle the blood").
- Verses 6 and 9—It was a sacrifice offered according to God's step-by-step plan; he had to skin (flay) the sacrificial animal and cut it into a number of pieces for the priest to put on the altar to be burned, some of which had to be washed and cleaned (the "inwards" and "legs").

- Verse 9—It was a sacrifice accepted by the Lord ("ofte made by fire" and a sweet and soothing savor or aroma to the Lord).

Now compare this with Christ's willingness to sacrifice Himself for us! Does this not make your head and heart—overwhelmed with unworthiness—bow in thanksgiving to your Lord for His willingness to present His body a sacrifice for you? I have to ask myself if I sacrifice to God with the same God-ordered mindset that pleased Him so many years ago.

- Do I sacrifice anything that actually costs me something (or do I simply give out of my reserve)?
- Do I sacrifice because I want to (or because I feel like I have to)?
- Do I sacrifice in a way that honors God with attention given to detail, purity, and completeness?

Which is your reasonable service (rational worship)

Reasonable (*logikeen*) means rational. It is a rational choice. It is a "thinking" kind of worship which is missing from the forced liturgy of a denominational worship or the Baptist been-there-done-that-here-we-go-again worship. It is a kind of worship that has nothing to do with the pilgrimage of a Muslim, the mandatory suffering of a Buddhist, the ritualism of a Roman Catholic, or the constrained church attendance of a Baptist. It is a rational reasoning based on the infinite mercy of a gracious God. Habituated worship must be thought through. Always remember that Christianity is to be focused on Christ and not on Christians. Are your worship services on Sundays "thought through" in a way that forces you to concentrate on Christ and what He has done for you?

Think about commentator Adam Clarke's words: "No thing can be more consistent with reason than that the work of God should glorify its Author. We are not our own; we are the property of the Lord, by the right of creation and redemption; and it would be as unreasonable as it would be wicked not to live for His glory, in strict obedience to His will."[4]

understand Worldly Conformity

> I beseech you therefore, brethren, by the mercies of God, that ye present your bodies a living sacrifice, holy, acceptable unto God, which is your reasonable service. And be not conformed to this world: but be ye transformed by the renewing of your mind, that ye may prove what is that good, and acceptable, and perfect, will of God. *(Romans 12:1–2)*

Paul challenges us with a tremendous goal in Romans 12:1. Now, in verse 2, he tells us how to accomplish that goal. As one commentator put it, he shows us what should be "shunned" and what should be "done."

And be not conformed to this world

And

The word *and* is a very important conjunction connecting two very important Bible principles. The *and* here reminds us that Paul is not finished explaining the devotion-driven duty we owe our wonderful Lord. He also wants us to realize that our willing, sacrificial commitment to Christ is to be couched in a nonconformist mindset. Along with the positive encouragement to willingly and sacrificially commit to God, there is a negative admonition to be not conformed to this present age.

Be not

Paul commands us to "be not conformed." He is encouraging us to stop something—and that something is worldly conformity. Just as we should be determined to do right, there are some things that we should passionately refuse. Our passionate refusal should be motivated by our passionate respect and reverence for our wonderful Savior.

And be not conformed

Once you have made up your mind to conform, it really is quite easy and takes very little thought. Like liquid Jell-O, you just simply ooze into the desired mold. You don't have to think to copy someone's behavior. Like art class in second grade, you just put a thin piece of white paper over a picture and start tracing. You don't have to think to follow worldly patterns, you just mimic what you see without thinking about how you get there or where it will lead you. Peter and Paul understood the danger of melting into a worldly mindset. Both writers use the same word, although in Romans 12:2, Paul's *syschematizo* is translated "conformed" and in 1 Peter 1:14, Peter's *syschematizo* is translated "fashioning." Whether it is the width of a belt, the style of hair, or the length of an outfit, the world's fashions change. The only thing constant about today's fashions is change. Again, to stay in style, it's quite easy and takes very little thought; just copy what everyone else is doing—whether it is good or bad! Just mimic others. Why could this non-thinking approach to life be so dangerous?

- Be not conformed—don't live "outside-in" but "inside-out."

- Be not conformed—let your inner attitudes affect your outer actions and not your outer actions influence your inner attitudes.
- Be not conformed—act your way into a new set of feelings; don't feel your way into a new set of actions.
- Be not conformed—it is not always a bad thing to be a nonconformist. Most people who rebel against a set of standards and refuse conformity choose a whole new set of standards to conform to. You often see this in dress as a teen nonconformist from a conservative background reacts and conforms to a new set of standards established by those they desire to be accepted by.

And be not conformed to this world

The world is ever changing. For instance, in our electronic world, about the time you get caught up on the maximum gigabytes, they find a way to double them. The day after you purchase a high-speed computer, a new model is introduced that triples the speed of the day-old computer you proudly own!

The philosophies of God's world and Satan's world illustrate this. God's kingdom is based on His character as revealed in His Word. I am thankful to say that some things never change: love, joy, peace, right, wrong, good, and bad. Satan's world is ever changing to that which is most convenient; he is a manipulator who changes the rules so he can win. You can see his approach in many historic denominational churches that keep changing their rules to recruit and retain new followers. A non-changing biblical philosophy of life based on the character of God is a wonderful mindset to base your life on. You can trust an unchanging Savior Who has proven His love and faithfulness for generations.

> *Every good gift and every perfect gift is from above, and cometh down from the Father of lights, with whom is no variableness, neither shadow of turning.* (James 1:17)

Jesus Christ the same yesterday, and to day, and for ever.
(Hebrews 13:8)

*For I am the Lord, I change not; therefore ye sons of Jacob
are not consumed.* (Malachi 3:6)

*I am Alpha and Omega, the beginning and the ending, saith
the Lord, which is, and which was, and which is to come, the
Almighty.* (Revelation 1:8)

*But this man, because he continueth ever, hath an un-
changeable priesthood. Wherefore he is able also to save
them to the uttermost that come unto God by him, seeing
he ever liveth to make intercession for them.* (Hebrews
7:24–25)

Believers should be nonconformists in relation to this ex-
ternal, non-lasting, fleeting philosophy of the age that we live
in. Don't let the word *philosophy* scare you. It simply means
"why we do what we do!" When Paul talks about this world,
he means much more than what we wear, what we listen to,
and how we choose to be entertained (although, all three of
these issues are sneak peaks of how much we are conformed
to this world's way of thinking). Those without Christ and
His Word think differently than do those who are committed to Christ. When you have some free time, compare the
following issues from the world's mindset and from a biblical
view.
- Submission to authority (Romans 13:1, Ephesians
  5:18–23, 1 Peter 5:5)
- Moral purity (1 Thessalonians 4:1–5, Proverbs 5–7,
  1 Corinthians 6:15–20)
- Lying, cheating, and deceit (Proverbs 12:22, John 8:44,
  John 14:6)
- Murder and abortion (Exodus 20:13, Galatians 5:19–21,
  Matthew 5:21–22)

The world approaches most issues much differently than
do those who are committed to the Word of God. The apostle

John's description of the world's mindset (the way the world thinks) has not changed since he penned these words:

> *Love not the world, neither the things that are in the world. If any man love the world, the love of the Father is not in him. For all that is in the world, the lust of the flesh, and the lust of the eyes, and the pride of life, is not of the Father, but is of the world. And the world passeth away, and the lust thereof: but he that doeth the will of God abideth for ever.* (1 John 2:15–17)

Remember, it's easy to conform—just refuse to think. Being a nonconformist to the world—refusing to think like the world thinks—is just another way of thanking our wonderful Lord for His love, forgiveness, and grace to us.

CHAPTER 17

Understand Godly Transformation

I beseech you therefore, brethren, by the mercies of God, that ye present your bodies a living sacrifice, holy, acceptable unto God, which is your reasonable service. And be not conformed to this world: but be ye transformed by the renewing of your mind, that ye may prove what is that good, and acceptable, and perfect, will of God. *(Romans 12:1–2)*

But be ye transformed by the renewing of your mind

As a child, I dreamed of being a cowboy, a pioneer explorer, and a professional baseball player, but never an English grammarian. Wrestling with dangling participles, verb tenses, and adverbial phrases was not my favorite sport. (Now I wish I knew more.) Therefore, I need to borrow brains from guys like Hendriksen and Kistemaker (New Testament Commentary Series) who can help explain difficult Bible passages. Here are Hendriksen's comments on Romans 12:2.[1]

1. Paul uses the present tense: "Continue to let your selves be transformed." Accordingly, this transformation must

not be a matter of impulse: on again, off again. It must be continuous.

2. The verb used is in the passive voice. Paul does not say, "Transform yourselves," but "Let yourselves be transformed." Transformation is basically the work of the Holy Spirit. It amounts to progressive sanctification. (2 Corinthians 3:18)

3. Nevertheless, the verb is in the imperative mood. Believers are not completely passive. Their responsibility is not canceled. They must allow the Spirit to do His work within their hearts and lives. Their duty is to cooperate to the full. (Philippians 2:12–13)

So an understanding of the present tense, the passive voice, and the imperative mood gives us a solid hold on Paul's intent to these young Romans. When it comes to a renewed mind and a transformed life, we need to get serious about our daily submission to the Holy Spirit's work in our lives. Knowing that God promises to do His part (transformation), are we willing to do our part?

Be ye transformed

The word used for *transformed* in the Greek is *metamorphoo*, which reminds us of our science term *metamorphosis*. What is the first thing that comes to your mind when you hear the words *transform* or *metamorphosis*? For most today, it will either be the transformation of a gross, ugly caterpillar into a beautiful butterfly or the Optimus Prime-type Transformer toy that can change itself from a robot to a tractor-trailer truck in seconds.

Being transformed is becoming something completely different from what you are. Interestingly, the root of this word is used only four times in our Bible: Once here in Romans 12:2; once in 2 Corinthians 3:18; and twice in reference to Christ's transfiguration in Matthew 17:2 and Mark 9:2. When Christ was transfigured in the presence of Peter, James, and John, He was transfigured before them, "and His face did shine as the sun, and His raiment was white as the light"

(Matthew 17:2). Right before these fishermen's eyes, Christ's earthly body was transformed to a heavenly body. His supernatural body glistened brightly and glowed like the blinding sun. It was a dramatic, visible change. Obviously, you don't walk around with a glowing halo over your head, but what visible change can others see in you since you yielded your life completely to Christ?

Paul encourages us in the transformation process when he wrote, "We all, with open face beholding as in a glass the glory of the Lord, are changed into the same image from glory to glory, even as by the Spirit of the Lord" (2 Corinthians 3:18). In other words, we are being transformed into the likeness of Jesus Christ day by day and step by step through the power of the Holy Spirit of God! God transforms us for His glory as we seek to biblically renew our minds.

By the renewing of your mind

There is no pill you can take for this. The renewing of the mind will never be accomplished with five minutes of prayer or drive-through-devos each morning. The renewal process is a minute-by-minute, hour-by-hour, day-by-day, week-by-week, month-by-month, year-by-year discipline to saturate your heart and mind with the Word of God. This must be your life practice.

Who wants a stale, musty, out-of-date, worn out, tired, grumpy, grouchy old mind?

To renew is to make new again. The newness of a baby's mind with its innocence, purity, and intense desire to learn is something to envy. If we can somehow clean out the entertainment garbage, the selfish reasonings, and the worldly thought processes, we will be on our way to both a renewed mind and a transformed life. To remodel an old house, you need to get rid of the old and replace it with new. In your mind, you need to replace hate with what? Lust with what? Anger with what? Fear with what? Selfishness with what? Pride with what? Laziness with what? Second Corinthians

4:16–18 and Colossians 3:10 give two very important principles regarding the renewing process. One gives us a key to what kind of knowledge we need and the other gives us a bit of a time-management concept on how this renewing process takes place. Look at each passage closely.

And have put on the new man, which is renewed in knowledge after the image of Him that created Him. (Colossians 3:10)

For which cause we faint not; but though our outward man perish, yet the inward man is renewed day by day. For our light affliction, which is but for a moment, worketh for us a far more exceeding and eternal weight of glory; while we look not at the things which are seen, but at the things which are not seen: for the things which are seen are temporal; but the things which are not seen are eternal. (2 Corinthians 4:16–18)

So, to remake, remodel, and make new the thoughts and attitudes of our selfish and immature minds, we need a consistent, step-by-step commitment to know more and more about our Creator, the Lord Jesus Christ. Remember, Colossians teaches us that Jesus Christ is the visible "icon" of the invisible God. Every time you learn something new about God's character, it will impact the way you think and live. What do you do on a daily basis to renew your mind?

So how can I thank God for delivering me from my sin? I must fervently renew my mind and watch my Lord transform my life into a life that pleases Him.

CHAPTER 18

Understand God's Will

I beseech you therefore, brethren, by the mercies
of God, that ye present your bodies a living
sacrifice, holy, acceptable unto God, which is
your reasonable service. And be not conformed
to this world: but be ye transformed by the
renewing of your mind, that ye may prove what
is that good, and acceptable, and perfect, will of
God. *(Romans 12:1–2)*

**That ye may prove what is that good, and acceptable, and
perfect will of God**

As we become less and less conformed to this world and
more and more transformed into the likeness of Jesus Christ
Himself, we will be more able to discern God's will for our
lives and be more prepared to display to others that the will
of God is perfect, acceptable, and very, very good. Have you
discerned what God's will is for your life? Discerning the will
of God takes some effort. You will not find it in a fortune
cookie at your favorite Chinese restaurant, the flip of a coin,
or written on your Facebook wall. In fact, if you have not
applied what we just read (refusing to accept the world's way
of thinking and instead, renewing and saturating your mind
with Scripture), you will probably have a hard time discerning God's will for your life.

Many of us, after failing a difficult algebra test or bombing an English grammar quiz, have considered quitting school. Now, if you quit the school of Scripture that talks about putting off selfish habits, or if you play hooky from the course on renewing your mind, you will never be able to pass the test of proving to yourself God's will for your life! Before we go on to discuss the three elements of God's will, think about how you are fulfilling the following spiritual obligations that are foundational in knowing and understanding the wonderful will of God.

- What are you doing daily to keep from being conformed to this world?
- What are you doing daily to renew your mind?
- How has God transformed your life in the last couple weeks?

That good, and acceptable, and perfect will of God

Although some of God's will is concealed, much of it is revealed. We must make sure we are honoring the revealed will of God before we can confidently expect to know His concealed will. What does God's Word already say about God's will? There are actually more than twenty New Testament references to the will of God. Do you confidently thank God for what He has done for you and honor your Lord through the purity of your own body? Do you do both from the heart? In a biblical nutshell, that is the will of God for your life.

> *Not with eyeservice, as menpleasers; but as the servants of Christ, doing the will of God from the heart; with good will doing service, as to the Lord, and not to men.* (Ephesians 6:6–7)

> *For this is the will of God, even your sanctification, that ye should abstain from fornication: that every one of you should know how to possess his vessel in sanctification and honor.* (1 Thessalonians 4:3–4)

In every thing give thanks: for this is the will of God in Christ Jesus concerning you. (1 Thessalonians 5:18)

God is pleased with a heart that desires purity and expresses thanksgiving. In a more general way, God's Word is God's will! Since God wants the best for our lives, He wants us to live according to His will (which is according to His Word). In Romans 12:2, Paul describes God's will with what three words? *Good, acceptable,* and *perfect.*

God's will is always good! In one word, it's profitable. Jesus spoke of good trees and good soil; Mary chose the good part at Jesus' feet; good things come from the heart of good men; good gifts come from a good God. Each use of the word *good* shows us something that is good as compared to bad, beneficial as compared to harmful, useful as compared to wasteful. God's will is always good! How has God already used your life's gifts for something good, and how do you envision Him using your spiritual gifts for good in the future?

God's will is always acceptable! In three words, it's pleasing to God. Here is a short, concise, personal testimony from our Lord Jesus as He lived on this earth: "He that sent Me is with Me . . . for I do always those things that please Him" (John 8:29). Paul then testifies of Christ in Romans 15:3 when he wrote, "Even Christ pleased not himself." We can choose to either please God (which is acceptable) or please self (which is totally unacceptable). In what ways have you pleased God (walked in His will) or displeased God (run from His will) in the past two weeks?

God's will is always perfect! It will produce God's intended purpose. The Greek root word for *perfect* is *teleios,* which has its own portfolio of word pictures. Meaning *full, complete,* or *finished, teleios* was used in 1 Corinthians 13:10, for *love* in 1 John 4:18, for the mature believer in Colossians 1:28, and for Christ's final words on the cross, "It is finished," in John 19:30. God has an intended purpose for your life that He wants to bring to a finish. Stay in His will and in His Word and watch Him accomplish His purpose in your life. To prove this, "be not conformed to this world but be ye transformed by the renewing of your mind" (Romans 12:2). What a wonderful way to thank God for His redemptive work in your life. He forgave you. He saved you.

Are you faithfully living in God's good, acceptable, and perfect will?

CHAPTER 19

Think! Think! Think!

For I say, through the grace given unto me, to every man that is among you, not to think of himself more highly than he ought to think; but to think soberly, according as God hath dealt to every man the measure of faith. *(Romans 12:3)*

Now here's a verse that gives us—every one of us—something to think about. God has an assignment for each one of us, and His purpose will be revealed through the grace-induced inner desires and giftedness He has given us. Different people think of different ways to handle different tasks. God has gifted (assigned) each one in His body the necessary gifts to fulfill the assigned tasks He has given. Not everyone is assigned the same task or gifted in the same way. No one task makes the doer any more special to God than another. We are simply to use the gifts and enablement that God has given to do what He wants us to do.

As Paul encourages us to stop and think—emphasizing both what "not to think" as well as what we "ought to think." He uses the root word *phroneo* four times in this forty-four-word, God-inspired sentence. Think, think, think, think! Most of us are either too tired to think, too busy to think, too lazy to think, or are happy to let someone else think for us! "Just tell me what to do. Don't make me think!" But God wants us to think! How? God tells us what we are not to think and what we ought to think. We are to think how He wants us to think . . . think soberly.

Not to think of himself more highly

We often pray, "Lord, I am nothing and worthless. Please use me in spite of me." Then when someone else calls us nothing or worthless, we get all bent out of shape. It might reveal that we are not being totally honest when we boast of nothingness to God! When we realize that any and every ability that we have has been gifted or given to us by God (that we did not deserve, earn, work for, or buy), how can there be any room for pride or arrogance? There are really no self-made men in the body of Christ. How can I get proud when it is all of God (through His grace) and none of me?

The Greek word *hyperphroneo* comes from the words *hyper,* which means "above" or "over," and *phroneo,* which means "to think". Combining these words produces "to think highly" or "consider something of great importance." Some think that they are Superman! Although they may not be faster than a speeding bullet or have the ability to leap tall buildings in a single bound, they do think they are super in the sense of being superior to others who are not as gifted, talented, or exceptional as they are. Do you know anyone who thinks he is more important to God than others? Do you think that because you are so special to God, He loves you more than anyone else on earth? Peter, one of Paul's friends, attacks such haughty thinking with these words:

> *Then Peter opened his mouth, and said, Of a truth I perceive that God is no respecter of persons.* (Acts 10:34)

> *And if ye call on the Father, who without respect of persons judgeth according to every man's work, pass the time of your sojourning here in fear.* (1 Peter 1:17)

Ought to think

We must think. It is necessary to think. It is inevitable to think once all the facts are in. How ought we to think about ourselves? Remember our study of Romans 1–3 as we examined the gravity of depravity? Honestly evaluate your motives, your thought life, your selfishness, your attitudes, and more. What ought you to think about yourself?

Commentator Donald Barnhouse encourages us to "think meek! Meekness is a vertical virtue, measuring self against God at every moment. It has nothing to do with the horizontal virtue that measures a man by other men."[1] As we compare ourselves with a holy, wonderful God, we are reminded that we "all have sinned" and fall way short of His glorious perfection.

But to think soberly

In the Greek New Testament, this phrase looks something like this, *alla phronein eis to sophronein*. If you notice, the word *phronein* appears twice. Literally, Paul is telling us to think with thinking that is sober, sane, discreet, discerning, and self-disciplined. It is actually the opposite of foolish, insane, undisciplined thinking. We are what we think. What we are thinking today we are becoming tomorrow. If we can think the way that God wants us to think, then we will live according to God's good, acceptable, and perfect will for our lives. On the other hand, if we are controlled by undisciplined, irrational, and foolish thoughts, we will displease our wonderful Lord. Specifically, God is reminding us to be totally honest in our self-appraisals. We can do this if we contemplate Paul's personal thoughts about himself:

> *Whereof I was made a minister, according to the gift of the grace of God given unto me by the effectual working of his power. Unto me, who am less than the least of all saints, is this grace given, that I should preach among the Gentiles the unsearchable riches of Christ.* (Ephesians 3:7–8)

Many struggle with what the world calls a low self-image. Although such thinking is quite popular and seems logical, this kind of thinking is very unbiblical. Don't be fooled with such thinking; remember, we are created by God, created in His image, created for His glory! Unreservedly we are given gifts by God: "according as God hath dealt to every man the measure of faith."

Let me repeat myself. God has an assignment for each one of us. His purpose will be revealed through His grace-induced inner desires and giftedness. God has gifted (assigned) each one in His body to fulfill the assigned tasks He has given. We are to simply use the gifts and enablement God has given us to do what He wants us to do. Now that is something to seriously think about.

CHAPTER 20

Accept Who You Are

For as we have many members in one body, and all members have not the same office: so we, being many, arc one body in Christ, and every one members one of another. *(Romans 12:4–5)*

We are all different. Very different! We have different gifts, different personalities, different backgrounds, different looks, different viewpoints, different opinions, different goals, and different dreams. We are all different because God created us that way. The astounding creativity and variety in God's creation can be seen in the plant world, the creatures of the sea, the animal world, and our world of man. We are all created in God's image, but there is only one of Him and many of us.

- Just how many members are in our bodies?
- What is the purpose of some of the uncomely parts (big toes, nose hairs, earlobes)?
- Are any members of my body insignificant, unnecessary, or worthless?
- Are any members of Christ's body insignificant, unnecessary, or worthless?
- What is my role or responsibility (office) in Christ's body?
- What is my responsibility to the other members of Christ's body?

- Since there are so many members, who should be in charge?

Our bodies are made up of many members or parts. How many? Well it depends on how specific or general you want to be. If you want to count each chromosome, go for it, but you had better have plenty of free time because there are forty-six chromosomes in each cell and humans have about one hundred trillion cells—give or take a few. Jewish tradition, according to the Talmud, says that the Jew was given 613 commandments (called the *mitzvoth*): 248 positive commands and 365 negative commands. The 365 negative commands match the number of days in a year, and some say that the 248 positive commands correspond to the number of parts of the human body. Interesting. Could this just happen? Is there any way that our ancient ancestors were sea creatures, blobs of primeval ooze, or second cousins to the orangutan family? Our bodies are amazing creations of God. God created the human brain that makes the latest electronic marvel pale in comparison. Next time someone attempts to convince you that you were a freakish act of some hiccup in nature, share with them the comfort of knowing that an all-knowing, all-powerful, kind, and loving God created you for His pleasure. If you need reminders of this, go to God's Word and dig from Genesis to Revelation to see who was behind our glorious world.

In the beginning God created the heaven and the earth. (Genesis 1:1)

And God said, Let us make man in our image, after our likeness: and let them have dominion over the fish of the sea, and over the fowl of the air, and over the cattle, and over all the earth, and over every creeping thing that creepeth upon the earth. (Genesis 1:26)

And God saw every thing that he had made, and, behold, it was very good. And the evening and the morning were the sixth day. (Genesis 1:31)

I have made the earth, and created man upon it: I, even my hands, have stretched out the heavens, and all their host have I commanded. (Isaiah 45:12)

For thus saith the Lord that created the heavens; God himself that formed the earth and made it; he hath established it, he created it not in vain, he formed it to be inhabited: I am the Lord; and there is none else. (Isaiah 45:18)

In the beginning was the Word, and the Word was with God, and the Word was God. The same was in the beginning with God. All things were made by him; and without him was not any thing made that was made. (John 1:1–3)

He was in the world, and the world was made by him, and the world knew him not. (John 1:10)

For by him were all things created, that are in heaven, and that are in earth, visible and invisible, whether they be thrones, or dominions, or principalities, or powers: all things were created by him, and for him: and he is before all things, and by him all things consist. (Colossians 1:16–17)

Thou art worthy, O Lord, to receive glory and honor and power: for thou hast created all things, and for thy pleasure they are and were created. (Revelation 4:11)

Knowing that there are many members to our bodies, you have to wonder if we could do without any. Do we really need big toes, nose hairs, and an appendix? Some say that the appendix is a hangout for good bacteria until it is needed. It would be hard to keep your balance without a big toe. Can you imagine the millions of ugly germs, spores, and pathogens that would fly up your nostrils without nose hairs? Nothing that God has orchestrated in your body is worthless, unnecessary, or insignificant. And neither are you to the body of Christ. Do you ever feel invisible or insignificant to God? If you do, how do you biblically attack those foolish thoughts? Psalm 139 is the classic passage that is both comforting and convicting when we start to question why God made us the way He did.

I will praise thee; for I am fearfully and wonderfully made: marvelous are thy works; and that my soul knoweth right well. My substance was not hid from thee, when I was made in secret, and curiously wrought in the lowest parts of the earth. Thine eyes did see my substance, yet being unperfect; and in thy book all my members were written, which in continuance were fashioned, when as yet there was none of them. How precious also are thy thoughts unto me, O God! How great is the sum of them! If I should count them, they are more in number than the sand: when I awake, I am still with thee. (Psalm 139:14–18)

Just as the nose and toes have different functions in the body, so do you and I. The word *office* in Romans 12:4 has the concept of doing or performing a certain action. Synonyms such as *role, function, job, responsibility,* or *task* help us to understand its meaning. So what is your office in the body of Christ? How has God gifted you to do your part? Remember, we are all different, and God made us that way. One way to thank God for rescuing us from our sin is to accept who and what we are and to live for His glory.

CHAPTER 21

Love One Another

For as we have many members in one body, and all members have not the same office: so we, being many, are one body in Christ, and every one members one of another. (Romans 12:4–5)

So, what is my responsibility to the other members of Christ's body? When Paul wrote that every one of us were members one of another, he was not just filling space in his letter with words. These words have a purpose that we cannot overlook or ignore. Being members one of another has the concept of all "belonging" to each other. Each part is concerned for the other parts. No part is superior or inferior. I understand author Donald Barnhouse's statement on this thought: "I minimize our differences in secondary matters and magnify the oneness that is ours because we have been taken out of the same pit, established on the same rock, and given the same song to sing."[1]

Now, we need to keep in mind the concept of biblical separation from those who are purposefully (or even without malice) violating scriptural principles for the sake of unity or numbers or acceptance. The ultimate goal is God's glory and not unity. Even the Lord said that a commitment to Him will cause division in families. I need to be fully persuaded in my mind that what I commit to is of God and worth causing

division. There will always be division between believers
and unbelievers, but what about division between believing brothers? If I take a stand against a believing brother on
a particular issue, I must be bottom-line, Bible-sure on that
issue. If I cannot be Bible-sure but sense its importance for
my own practical holiness, I will live by the principle in my
own life and ministry, but I do not have to insist that everyone has to agree with me. I can even separate without making
a public announcement of my decision.

God uses the phrase "one another" in many ways with
varied applications. By studying the "one anothers" in
Scripture we can understand how Jesus Christ wants us to
treat each other.

*A new commandment I give unto you, That ye love one another; as I have loved you, that ye also love one another. By
this shall all men know that ye are my disciples, if ye have
love one to another.* (John 13:34–35)

*Be kindly affectioned one to another with brotherly love; in
honour preferring one another.* (Romans 12:10)

*Wherefore receive ye one another, as Christ also received us
to the glory of God.* (Romans 15:7)

*And I myself also am persuaded of you, my brethren, that ye
also are full of goodness, filled with all knowledge, able also
to admonish one another.* (Romans 15:14)

*For, brethren, ye have been called unto liberty; only use not
liberty for an occasion to the flesh, but by love serve one
another.* (Galatians 5:13)

With all lowliness and meekness, with longsuffering, forbearing one another in love. (Ephesians 4:2)

*And be ye kind one to another, tenderhearted, forgiving one
another, even as God for Christ's sake hath forgiven you.*
(Ephesians 4:32)

Forbearing one another, and forgiving one another, if any man have a quarrel against any: even as Christ forgave you, so also do ye. (Colossians 3:13)

Wherefore comfort one another with these words. (1 Thessalonians 4:18)

Wherefore comfort yourselves together, and edify one another, even as also ye do. (1 Thessalonians 5:11)

For this is the message that ye heard from the beginning, that we should love one another. (1 John 3:11)

Paul dealt with this very same issue with the young and struggling Corinthian believers, telling them in 1 Corinthians 12:25 that there should be no division in the body but that the members should genuinely care for each other.

We trust that Christ would be pleased with the way we love, prefer, receive, admonish, serve, forbear, forgive, comfort, and edify both our agreeing and disagreeing brothers in Christ.

We have to be careful that we do not take lightly the unity of the body of Christ. Unity is not something to be ignored. I think too many popular table games have wormed their way into our thinking and affected our desire for biblical unity today.

- **Monopoly**—We have a monopoly on truth; no one else has truth but us. We are right and all others are wrong.
- **Trouble**—If you are moving, I'll do what I can to stop you. I will win and you will lose.
- **Trivial Pursuit**—Spending time trying to answer foolish questions that will not make us any smarter or any godlier is a trivial pursuit par excellence.
- **Mouse Trap/Kaboom/Jenga**—Some things you simply don't touch. If you push or pull the wrong thing, watch out for an explosion.

Since there are so many members, who is in charge? Paul does not explain the headship of Christ in Romans 12, but it is necessary to remind ourselves that Christ is the head of the body and should be in control of each and every member; that no member should strive to have preeminence over any other members; and that if each member of the body is motivated by love, the body of Christ will mature and grow into a healthy, loving body. Paul made sure that both the Ephesian and Colossian Christians knew both Christ's role as the head of the body and their role as individual members in His body.

> But speaking the truth in love, may grow up into Him in all things, which is the head, even Christ: from whom the whole body fitly joined together and compacted by that which every joint supplieth, according to the effectual working in the measure of every part, maketh increase of the body unto the edifying of itself in love. (Ephesians 4:15–16)

> And [Christ] is before all things, and by him all things consist. And he is the head of the body, the church: who is the beginning, the firstborn from the dead; that in all things he might have the preeminence. (Colossians 1:17–18)

> These things I command you, that ye love one another. (John 15:17)

CHAPTER 22

Thank God for His Grace Gifts

Having then gifts differing according to the grace that is given to us, whether prophecy, let us prophesy according to the proportion of faith; or ministry, let us wait on our ministering: or he that teacheth, on teaching; or he that exhorteth, on exhortation: he that giveth, let him do it with simplicity; he that ruleth, with diligence; he that sheweth mercy, with cheerfulness. *(Romans 12:6–8)*

The Giver

Actually, this is the second time Paul deals with God, grace, and gifts in this chapter. Just three verses earlier Paul encouraged us "to think soberly, according as God hath dealt to every man the measure of faith" (Romans 12:3). As we compare that phrase with "having then gifts differing according to the grace that is given to us" (Romans 12:6), and ask counsel from Peter, we get a better idea of what is being taught here.

As every man hath received the gift, even so minister the same one to another, as good stewards of the manifold grace of God. If any man speak, let him speak as the oracles of God; if any man minister, let him do it as of the ability which God giveth: that God in all things may be glorified through Jesus Christ, to whom be praise and dominion for ever and ever. Amen. (1 Peter 4:10–11)

- We are all different, with different gifts and different abilities. God did that.
- God, by His grace, has given us different gifts to do certain things well.
- Our gracious God has enabled us with specific gifts. Let's use them for His glory!
- Focus on using your gift and refuse to focus on the misuse of others' gifts.
- Remember, they are gifts! Gifts are unearned and undeserved.
- God is the Giver.
- God, as the Giver, gives grace which enables us to use our gifts.
- God, as the Giver, has given specific gifts to you that, through His grace, you will use to glorify His name.
- God is the One Who chooses who gets what gift or how many gifts.
- God is the One Who enables the getter to use the gift that he got.
- God is the One Who should get the glory (and not the getter).

The Grace

Paul begins his warning to those gifted by God by saying, "For I say, through the grace given unto me" (Romans 12:3). He wanted all to know that he could not have written his prophetic, confrontational exhortation to stay humble aside from the grace of God. It seems that some people value certain gifts as better than others and are proud if they have a showier gift. Why is it much easier to stay humble using the gifts of serving or giving than of preaching and leading?

Now, the reason we have gifts, the reason we have different gifts, and the reason we have different degrees of different gifts is according to the grace that is given to us. Peter uses the phrase "the manifold grace of God," which could be translated "God's varied grace," "God's grace in various forms," or "God's grace given in a multitude of colors" (like the variegated yarn my grandma used to use, which included every color in the rainbow). Don't worry about what color of a gift you got or how much of that gift you received, just use your giftedness to serve Christ and to love others to Christ. Grace can be defined as divine enablement. God not only gives you the gift but the ability to use it properly.

A half-full, ten-thousand-gallon tank looks much more impressive than a small pint jar that is full and running over. Don't let the size of the container impress you or discourage you. Determine what size tank or jar you are, commit it totally to the Lord, and let it overflow. As you spill all over the place, you will impact lives for God's glory.

Every believer is gifted by God. Some, through the habit of selfish thinking, may believe that they are incredibly gifted above all others; and others, still through habitual selfish thinking, believe that they have received no gifts from God. Both manifestations of selfish thinking are unbiblical and displeasing to God. God gifted you to serve Him in a unique and special way. Although Paul deals with other gifts and talents in Ephesians 4 and 1 Corinthians 12, he lists here seven gifts that God has given for the purpose of using godly people to help other people be godly. Thank God for the gifts He has given you and for the gifts He has given others for your benefit.

CHAPTER 23

Use Your Gifts for God

The Gifts

James 1:17 reminds us that all good gifts come from God, our unchanging heavenly Father. A gift is just that. A gift! You don't work for a gift; you can't earn a gift; you never pay the giver back for a gift; you don't deserve a gift. As seen in Romans 12:6–8, God looked down over His entire church and knew what gifts were necessary to help them grow and mature in Christ. He listed the gifts of prophecy, serving, teaching, encouraging, giving, leading, and kindly showing mercy. In what way has God gifted you, and how are you using those gifts to encourage others? If you are not sure, think through each gift and see how God has already gifted you in one or more of these areas. Meditate on how God might want to use you and your gift for His glory and the good of others.

Prophesy

"Let us prophesy according to the proportion of faith" (Romans 12:6). Speak out with as much faith as God has given, but no more.

Preach the Word! Give the truth of God, with the love of God, so that lives are changed for the glory of God.

In answer to the question "Who is this?" in Matthew 21:10, the multitude said, "This is Jesus the *prophet* of Nazareth of Galilee." In our endeavor to be like Christ, we must not ignore growing in this gift of prophecy.

There are two ways to look at prophesying: either it is a foretelling of the truth or a forth-telling of the truth. Today, we have the complete, sufficient Word of God. We do not need or should not seek "new" truth. Paul reminds us that true modern-day prophesying must include three elements: edification, exhortation, and comfort. In 1 Corinthians 14:3 Paul wrote, "He that prophesieth speaketh unto men to edification, and exhortation, and comfort." If a man is a God-called prophesier, he will be both patient and biblical.

Preach the word; be instant in season, out of season; reprove, rebuke, exhort with all longsuffering and doctrine. (2 Timothy 4:2)

God further explained the goal of New Testament prophesying as He inspired Paul to deal with the issue of tongues in the church at Corinth: our preaching should build up, encourage, and console!

Follow after charity, and desire spiritual gifts, but rather that ye may prophesy. For he that speaketh in an unknown tongue speaketh not unto men, but unto God: for no man understandeth him; howbeit in the spirit he speaketh mysteries. But he that prophesieth speaketh unto men to edification, and exhortation, and comfort. He that speaketh in an unknown tongue edifieth himself; but he that prophesieth edifieth the church. I would that ye all spake with tongues, but rather that ye prophesied: for greater is he that prophesieth than he that speaketh with tongues, except he interpret, that the church may receive edifying. (1 Corinthians 14:1–5)

Minister

"Let us wait on our ministering" (Romans 12:7a). We are never more Christlike than when we serve. Serve well with a servant's heart. Serve because you want to and because you find joy in doing so, not because you have to or find acceptance in doing so.

There are capital *M* ministers and little *m* ministers. Our Lord Jesus Christ came to earth as a little *m* minister.

Jesus chose to be a servant. Philippians 2:2–8 describes the mind of a servant, while John 13:4–17 illustrates the actions of a servant. Jesus willingly, joyfully, sacrificially, and humbly served. When you read through those passages, you will realize that our Lord did not serve out of duty, because of guilt, or for gain. Those who possess the gift of serving also possess character traits such as dependability, initiative, and perseverance. They seem to know what needs to be done and do it! They prepare the surroundings to make it easy for those preaching, teaching, or counseling to use their gifts without distractions.

> *But it shall not be so among you: but whosoever will be great among you, let him be your minister; and whosoever will be chief among you, let him be your servant: even as the Son of man came not to be ministered unto, but to minister, and to give His life a ransom for many.* (Matthew 20:26–28)

> *He riseth from supper, and laid aside His garments; and took a towel, and girded Himself. After that He poureth water into a bason, and began to wash the disciples' feet, and to wipe them with the towel wherewith he was girded.* (John 13:4–5)

Teach

"Or he that teacheth, on teaching" (Romans 12:7*b*). Be fully prepared so that your students will not only receive knowledge, but the understanding behind the knowledge. Teach because you are driven to do so, not because you don't know what else to do. Teach because you are driven to do so and for no other reason.

Donald Grey Barnhouse in his commentary on Romans states, "When you receive a blessing from the Word of God, pass it on at once. When you learn something from a sermon, tell two or three other people at the earliest possible opportunity. Above all, apply the teaching to your own heart first; thus it comes to the listener with the impact of Heaven and the warmth of your own experience."[1]

Don't forget the Holy Spirit's reproof to the Hebrew Christians in Hebrews 5 when He reminded them that they seemed slow in grasping spiritual truth and should have already been teaching others but were still struggling with the ABCs of God's Word. Let the Holy Spirit of God use the holy Word of God to teach you how to be holy so you can teach others to be holy also.

> *Of whom we have many things to say, and hard to be uttered, seeing ye are dull of hearing. For when for the time ye ought to be teachers, ye have need that one teach you again which be the first principles of the oracles of God; and are become such as have need of milk, and not of strong meat. For every one that useth milk is unskilful in the word of righteousness: for he is a babe. But strong meat belongeth to them that are of full age, even those who by reason of use have their senses exercised to discern both good and evil.* (Hebrews 5:11–14)

CHAPTER 24

Encourage Others, Give to Others, and Lead Others

Exhort

"He that exhorteth, on exhortation" (Romans 12:8*a*). Encourage both by your life and by the Scriptures. Live with a contagious passion to help others see God more clearly and understand His ways more perfectly.

Be an encourager

When your friends become discouraged, be the one used by God to put the courage back into their lives. Exhort, support, back, and promote them. Believe in them, campaign for them, and be a spiritual fan who never misses a game—one who is always there to cheer from the sidelines. Encourage both by your life and by the Scriptures. Live with a contagious passion to help others see God more clearly and understand His ways more perfectly. The Greek word for *exhort* is *parakleet* (not *parakeet*), which literally means "to call alongside of" for help. Whom (it could be many) has God called you to go alongside of to help and encourage in their walk with God? Who is your exhorter? Who encourages you to be in God's Word and grow on a regular basis?

Jesus was a comforting exhorter to the diseased woman who touched His robe when He said, "Daughter, be of good comfort; thy faith hath made thee whole" (Matthew 9:22). Jesus wants to comfort and encourage us! Encourage!

Stay encouraged by God so you can be used of God to encourage others.

> *But exhort one another daily, while it is called To day; lest any of you be hardened through the deceitfulness of sin.* (Hebrews 3:13)

Encourage when you can because we have no idea when our time will be over on this earth and we cannot.

> *Not forsaking the assembling of ourselves together, as the manner of some is; but exhorting one another: and so much the more, as ye see the day approaching.* (Hebrews 10:25)

In some way, our reproofs, rebukes, and exhortations should be wrapped in encouragement before we give them to others.

> *Preach the word; be instant in season, out of season; reprove, rebuke, exhort with all longsuffering and doctrine.* (2 Timothy 4:2)

Give

"He that giveth, let him do it with simplicity" (Romans 12:8*b)*. Give with single-minded generosity and without any ulterior motives. If God has given to you, give without expecting more, give without feelings of being used, give because you find joy and peace in giving. Give with simple mental honesty: no pretending; no hypocrisy; no desire for recognition, a plaque, or a public show.

Give willingly. Give generously. Give liberally. Give to meet the needs of the needy. Be a giver. Give from the heart. Give without expecting anything in return. Give to others as God has given to you. The word *simplicity* reveals the simple purity of mind and sincerity of heart that is devoid of any ulterior motive. It explains the heart of the widow woman in Luke 21:1–4.

> *And He looked up, and saw the rich men casting their gifts into the treasury. And He saw also a certain poor widow casting in thither two mites. And He said, Of a truth I say unto you, that this poor widow hath cast in more than they all: for all these have of their abundance cast in unto the offerings of God: but she of her penury hath cast in all the living that she had.* (Luke 21:1–4)

Jesus certainly was gifted in giving. He gave the ultimate.

> *Who gave Himself for our sins, that He might deliver us from this present evil world, according to the will of God and our Father.* (Galatians 1:4)

Never forget our Lord's promise in the Gospel of Luke.

> *Give, and it shall be given unto you; good measure, pressed down, and shaken together, and running over, shall men give into your bosom. For with the same measure that ye mete withal it shall be measured to you again.* (Luke 6:38)

Lead

"He that ruleth, with diligence" (Romans 12:8*c*). Diligently take your leadership seriously. Know where you are going, how you are going to get there, and what you expect when you arrive. Be more than a good leader, be a *great* leader.

Real men (real leaders) race toward problems and try to fix them.

Lead. Be a leader. In a way, we are all leaders. We are either drawing others closer to our Lord or driving them farther away. The concept of diligence (*spoude*) clarifies a true leader's approach to life. When you meditate on the words *speed, urgency, hasten, earnestness,* and *zeal,* you should get an idea of the personality of diligence. *Diligence* is an action word. Action is the enemy of apathy.

Jesus was a leader. When He said, "Follow me!" (Matthew 16:24; Mark 10:21; Luke 9:23; John 12:26), He was giving an invitation for all to accept Him as the leader of their lives.

Peter reminds us of the attitude of leadership we should possess if we are going to be biblical, godly leaders:

Feed the flock of God which is among you, taking the oversight thereof, not by constraint, but willingly; not for filthy lucre, but of a ready mind; neither as being lords over God's heritage, but being ensamples to the flock. (1 Peter 5:2–3)

Show kindness

"He that sheweth mercy, with cheerfulness" (Romans 12:8*d).* Do it gladly, cheerfully because you want to and not because you have to (no martyr's complex, please). Be merciful to others because of the mercy that God has shown to you; do not be merciful so you can receive mercy from others.

Be cheerful. Show kindness. Mercy is motivated by pity. Pity for those with spiritual needs is not just feeling sorry for them, but it is a willingness to remove their miseries from them. Our Lord Jesus Christ removed our miseries by dying for us; we can help to remove the miseries of others by living for them. Whom can you encourage (by removing a tear from their eyes and putting a smile in their hearts) today?

How many have cried to the Lord, "Have mercy on me!" and received it? Most of us. So, if you cheerfully encourage others by sincerely giving of yourself and leading them closer to our merciful God, you are using your God-given gifts— just like Christ! Be a merciful, cheerful encourager, giver, and leader. Just like your Lord!

And be ye kind one to another, tenderhearted, forgiving one another, even as God for Christ's sake hath forgiven you. (Ephesians 4:32)

CHAPTER 25

Practice Genuine Love

The ten verses in Romans 12:9–18 simply encourage us to behave like Christians. We are to love, labor, live, and let live in a way that pleases God and is unquestionably loving to man. A simple breakdown of these verses shows four mandates of what to do and three practical principles of how to do so.

- Love
  1—honestly
  2—purely
  3—kindly
- Labor
  1—diligently
  2—biblically
  3—respectfully
- Live
  1—cheerfully
  2—patiently
  3—prayerfully
- Let live
  1—generously
  2—humbly
  3—peaceably

Let love be without dissimulation. Abhor that which is evil; cleave to that which is good. (Romans 12:9)

The thoughts and practical admonitions in Romans 12:9 have been translated or paraphrased in expressions such as:

- *Let love be without hypocrisy. Abhor what is evil. Cling to what is good.* (NKJV)
- *Let love be genuine. Abhor what is evil; hold fast to what is good.* (ESV)
- *Love must be sincere. Hate what is evil; cling to what is good.* (NIV)
- *Don't just pretend to love others. Really love them. Hate what is wrong. Hold tightly to what is good.* (NLT)
- *Love from the center of who you are; don't fake it. Run for dear life from evil; hold on for dear life to good.* (Hummel)

Let your love be real by sincerely hating the evil that could destroy the loved one's life and consistently clinging to the good that could encourage the loved one's heart. If someone questions if you are for real, they will see their answer in the way that you hate evil and cling to good. Don't just pretend that you love others, really love them.

"Without dissimulation" is another way of saying, "No hypocrisy allowed." The Greek word *hypokrites* is the root from where we get our word *hypocrisy*. Today, teens and adults alike are looking for reality. There is way too much "faking it" in our relationships with God and others. Most of us know when someone is genuine or not. God wants us to live with real love, real faith, and real wisdom.

Let your love be real!

Seeing ye have purified your souls in obeying the truth through the Spirit unto unfeigned love of the brethren, see that ye love one another with a pure heart fervently. (1 Peter 1:22)

Let your faith be real!

When I call to remembrance the unfeigned faith that is in thee, which dwelt first in thy grandmother Lois, and thy mother Eunice; and I am persuaded that in thee also. (2 Timothy 1:5)

Let your wisdom be real!

> *But the wisdom that is from above is first pure, then peace-*
> *able, gentle, and easy to be entreated, full of mercy and good*
> *fruits, without partiality, and without hypocrisy.* (James 3:17)

Before I can determine whether my love for others is genuine, I have to inspect my heart to see if my love for God is real. Take the time to slowly read Mark 12:30–31, and then ask yourself if you possess all four of the characteristics of sincere love and real commitment that John Mark lists for us.

> *And thou shalt love the Lord thy God with all thy heart,*
> *and with all thy soul, and with all thy mind, and with all*
> *thy strength: this is the first commandment. And the second*
> *is like, namely this, Thou shalt love thy neighbor as thyself.*
> *There is none other commandment greater than these.*
> (Mark 12:30–31)

Do I sincerely love God with **all my heart**? Are there other loves competing for first place in my heart? Am I wholeheartedly and willfully determined to love my God?

Do I sincerely love God with **all my soul**? This is the emotional part of our love as Christ's soul was deeply grieved while He prayed at Gethsemane. Does my selfishness grieve my heart as much as it grieves my Lord's?

Do I sincerely love God with **all my mind**? What I allow to consume and control my thoughts is what I truly care about. What I think about the most is what I love the most.

Do I sincerely love God with **all my strength**? Do I drain my energies for myself or for my God? As age increases and strength decreases, can I look back without regrets on how I have used my strength?

Abhor that which is evil

To honestly and sincerely love God as He loves me, I must hate sin as He hates sin. God reminds us in Psalm 97:10, "Ye that love the Lord, hate evil!" We have to ask ourselves some serious questions.

- Do I utterly detest or view with horror that which displeases God?

- Do I seek to separate from evil?
- Do I truly hate trivial sins as well as great sins?
- Do I sincerely hate the secret sins in my life as well as possible public sins?

Cleave to that which is good

To honestly and sincerely love God as He loves me, I must view good in a 1 Thessalonians way:

See that none render evil for evil unto any man; but ever follow that which is good. (1 Thessalonians 5:15)

It is easier to follow after good if you cleave to it. To cleave is to glue or cement yourself to something or someone. There are some glues that solvents can't touch. When we are super glued to good things, good people, or good works, solvents like peer pressure, public acceptance, and laziness cannot remove us from such good.

Let love be without dissimulation. Abhor that which is evil; cleave to that which is good. (Romans 12:9)

Since this is the way I am to love God, it would make sense that God wants me to love others with the same unselfish love.

CHAPTER 26

Love and Honor Others

Be kindly affectioned one to another with brotherly love; in honor preferring one another. (Romans 12:10)

Most of us are born with a competitive nature. Most want to win and few love to lose. In a way, this simple verse of fourteen English words (only nine words in the original Greek) is issuing a challenge to each of us to love each other with a brotherly affection—which sometimes is a challenge in itself. We should prefer, more easily understand, or outdo one another in showing such love and honor to each other. As we accept the challenge to engage in some friendly competition, what are the rules and how do you know if you win or lose?

"Be kindly affectioned (with brotherly love) one to another" (Romans 12:10). Love each other with the genuine affection that should be seen in family relationships. This brotherly love is so unique that to explain it, God had to make up a word that is not found in ordinary Greek. Sad to say, selfishness has crawled into our homes in tsunamic proportions, and many brothers and sisters have never experienced the kind of love that Paul is talking about here. Even some parents are so in love with themselves that they have lost the innate, natural love that even the animal kingdom expresses within its own families.

It is almost like God, through many writers of Scripture, assumes that all of us understand the loving, kind, quality relationships that we should have toward our family members.

Like as a father pitieth his children, so the Lord pitieth them that fear Him. (Psalm 103:13)

For whom the Lord loveth He correcteth; even as a father the son in whom he delighteth. (Proverbs 3:12)

But we were gentle among you, even as a nurse [young nursing mother] cherisheth her children. (1 Thessalonians 2:7)

Ye know how we exhorted and comforted and charged every one of you, as a father doth his children. (1 Thessalonians 2:11)

But as touching brotherly love ye need not that I write unto you: for ye yourselves are taught of God to love one another. (1 Thessalonians 4:9)

Let brotherly love continue. (Hebrews 13:1)

Do any of these verses convict you? Do you pity instead of attack; delight in rather than cut down; cherish rather than ignore; comfort rather than irritate; love rather than dislike? God tells us to love those we live with and to prefer them above ourselves.

In our selfish world today, too few love one another with brotherly love. Someone needs to take the lead and set an example for others to follow! Always be a step ahead. Don't follow the crowd. Be an example. Be a pacesetter. It is almost a contest to see who can outdo the other in showing honor and giving preference. Now, the only way that we can honestly and genuinely esteem others above ourselves is twofold: refuse to judge their motives and keep a humble view of (judge) our own heart. We do not know what is in the hearts of others and hardly understand what motivates our own hearts.

Refuse to judge the motives of others

First Corinthians 2:11 asks who can know a person's thoughts except that person's own spirit. We cannot read minds and therefore have no right attacking those who disagree with us on preferential issues. Before you attack others, ask others. Explain and apply the wise counsel found in Proverbs 1:5, "A wise man [husband, wife, parent, child, friend] will hear [take time to listen and take the energy to understand the opposing side of an issue], and will increase learning; and a man of understanding shall attain unto wise counsels."

Keep a humble view of your own heart

A careful look at how the publican viewed his own heart in Luke 18:13 and Paul's personal view of himself in Romans 7:24 combined with David's admission of his walk with God in Psalm 119:176 help us to understand how we should view our own hearts.

> *And the publican, standing afar off, would not lift up so much as his eyes unto heaven, but smote upon his breast, saying, God be merciful to me a sinner.* (Luke 18:13)

> *O wretched man that I am! Who shall deliver me from the body of this death?* (Romans 7:24)

> *I have gone astray like a lost sheep; seek thy servant; for I do not forget thy commandments.* (Psalm 119:176)

An honest appraisal of the depravity of our own hearts is essential to walking humbly with our God and preferring others above ourselves. It is not natural to put others first in our "me-first" world. Mr. and Mrs. Haughtypride put on a good front, love the front seats, the front of lines, and the front pages. But just because we look squeaky-clean does not mean we are clean all the way through. We can put on a good front and be totally wicked in everything hidden behind the façade. Never forget the Lord Jesus Christ's words to those who were visibly clean but refused to admit the depravity of their own hearts.

> *Woe unto you, scribes and Pharisees, hypocrites! For ye are like unto whited sepulchres, which indeed appear beautiful outward, but are within full of dead men's bones, and of all uncleanness. Even so ye also outwardly appear righteous unto men, but within ye are full of hypocrisy and iniquity.* (Matthew 23:27–28)

Have you ever considered what you would be capable of doing if given the perfect opportunity to sin with the promise of no one knowing and no consequences? Remember, at the foot of the cross, we are all wicked, selfish sinners in need of forgiveness. All men are born in the same depraved state.

CHAPTER 27

Serve God With an Enthusiastic, Fervent Attitude

Not slothful in business; fervent in spirit; serving the Lord. *(Romans 12:11)*

Most of those redeemed and freed from their sins want to serve the Lord and thank Him for delivering them from their enslaving sin. Some serve because they have to. Some serve because they feel a duty to. Then there are those who serve Him and others with a fervent, zealous, outrageous, contagious enthusiasm! Serve out of love and you will love to serve. Combine a fervent, inward attitude with diligent outward action, and you will have a true, biblical, fervent servant of God. Romans 12:10–12 gives a list of ten ways to serve others; verse 11 focuses on just three of them.

Not slothful in business

Don't be lazy. Never be lacking in zeal. Enjoy working hard. Work in such a way that you get tired on purpose. Laziness seems to be best friends with apathy and indifference.

If laziness were a poison, diligence would be its antidote. If apathy were a disease, fervency would be its cure. If indifference were a math problem, enthusiastic intensity would be its solution. People often forget what we say and what we do, but they will never forget our spirits and attitudes. There is nothing attractive about laziness. There is nothing about apathetic indifference that would cause anyone to want to know Christ more.

The phrase "not slothful in business" is interesting to dissect. The word *slothful* (*okneros*) means "to be slow," "to delay," "to be tardy," or "to be late." Synonyms such as *heavy, burdensome, tiresome, slow, sluggish,* and *inactive* help to describe the word's intent. The word *business* (*spoude*) has basically the very opposite meaning. It means "to speed," "to hasten," "to hurry up," "to earnestly and zealously attack a project or a problem." In a way, the entire phrase is saying, "Don't slow down your speed." Someone addicted to apathy would slothfully and lazily lag behind those who earnestly, fervently, and zealously attack life's challenges.

Diligence does not understand laziness. If diligence is looking at each opportunity in life as a special assignment from the Lord and using every ounce of energy to accomplish it, how would diligence view laziness? Laziness is in essence a lack of whatever it takes to work hard, to work fast, and to work long. So what causes us to be lazy? When we give in to laziness, what are we missing or lacking in life? It may not always be volitional, but how does a lack of restful sleep affect laziness in your life? How could a lack of exercise and stamina influence whether you approach a task with a lazy heart or a diligent spirit? How could a lack of commitment impact laziness? How could a lack of spiritual desire to please God affect your laziness? Laziness is a very popular sin overlooked by many but never overlooked by God.

Fervent in spirit

Someone has said that 80 percent of life is attitude. Our attitude or spirit in life is long remembered after what we say is forgotten. Paul is encouraging us to be fervent in spirit, which should convey a seething, scalding, boiling-hot attitude toward serving Christ. Being fervent in spirit implies that this zeal has to come from the heart! It cannot be a fake frothing at the mouth emotional pretense, but must be real heart fervency. Keep your spiritual fervor. Simply care enough to let it grab hold of your heart in such a way you are totally committed and enthusiastically involved. How do you keep such fervency of heart day after day? Simply remind yourself that we have ruined our lives in sin, that God's remedy is Jesus Christ, and that we should live our lives in a way that thanks God for what He has done for us! Remember, we have ruined our lives in sin; God's remedy is Jesus Christ. So how can we live our lives in a way that thanks God for what He has done for us? How will a faith-filled visit to the cross keep you fervent, hot, and intensely committed to serving your Lord? Think about what you were before Calvary and what you are after Calvary, and you will have your answer.

Serving the Lord

We are never more Christlike than when we serve. A servant's heart was the heart of our Savior. Paul clearly explained this in his letter to the Philippians.

> Let this mind be in you, which was also in Christ Jesus: who, being in the form of God, thought it not robbery to be equal with God: but made Himself of no reputation, and took upon Him the form of a servant, and was made in the likeness of men: and being found in fashion as a man, He humbled Himself, and became obedient unto death, even the death of the cross. (Philippians 2:5–8)

Jesus clearly portrayed this when He personally chose to do what the house servant normally did and washed the feet of His disciples (John 13:1–17). None of the twelve volunteered, but Jesus did. Most were probably just not thinking. They would have been willing if asked, but it did not come to mind. That is one of the differences between a true servant and a person willing to serve. The true servant looks for a task to do, no matter how menial, and does it. Take a minute and read through John 13:1–17 and meditate on the example that Christ left for all of us to follow.

When you look closely at what the Word of God says about serving, you'll be faced with some very thought-provoking issues to deal with.

- Serving can be spiritually, emotionally and physically draining.

  Serving the Lord with all humility of mind, and with many tears, and temptations. (Acts 20:19a)

- Serving involves *all* your heart and soul.

  What doth the Lord thy God require of thee . . . to serve the Lord thy God with all thy heart and with all thy soul. (Deuteronomy 10:12–13)

- Serving is a choice.

  And if it seem evil unto you to serve the Lord, choose you this day whom ye will serve . . . but as for me and my house, we will serve the Lord. (Joshua 24:15)

- Serving involves a wholesome dread of apathetic serving and an overwhelming awe of whom we have the privilege to serve.

  Serve the Lord with fear, and rejoice with trembling. (Psalm 2:11)

CHAPTER 28

Patiently Rejoice and Continually Pray

Rejoicing in hope; patient in tribulation; continuing instant in prayer. *(Romans 12:12)*

With a merry and joyful heart motivated by what will be in the future, don't give in to what has been in the past, and don't give up to what is presently troubling you today. Be devoted to prayer—thanking God for what He has allowed in the past and trusting God for both what He is permitting in the present and providing for the future.

Rejoicing in hope

Chairo is the Greek word for rejoicing, gladness, or joy. A "chairo attitude" is the best way to pick up the heavy burdens of life and successfully carry them to the end of life.

Is any among you afflicted? Let him pray. Is any merry? Let him sing psalms. (James 5:13)

Biblical hope is not the hope of an "I hope I make it" or an "I hope so" lifestyle, but the happy anticipation and joyful eagerness of experiencing first hand what our Lord has in store for us. We know that He is preparing a place for us

(John 14:1–3) and that no one can even imagine the things that God is preparing for those who love Him (1 Corinthians 2:9). Those are both wonderful truths to have hope in.

Patient (persevering) in tribulation

Those who possess patient endurance can persevere under the heavy loads of life without complaining, griping, or giving up. If an admiring young man volunteers to carry a backpack full of books for that special young lady, he will carry that heavy load (without complaint or protest) as far as she needs. Many today carry heavily loaded backpacks full of miseries, adversities, persecutions, and difficulties that are much too heavy to carry without the strength supplied by an almighty, sustaining God. If you had to make a check list of the heavy load in your personal backpack, what difficulties and trials would weigh it down? Is what you carry too heavy for God? Does God lack the power, might, or desire to help you with such burdens? Those who are patient in tribulation will not be constantly looking to unload those burdens but will persevere by willingly carrying the weight until God lightens the heavy load.

In regard to burdens and difficulties that we are called to carry, one of the most encouraging passages of Scripture I have ever studied is found at the end of 2 Corinthians 4.

> *For which cause we faint not; but though our outward man perish, yet the inward man is renewed day by day. For our light affliction, which is but for a moment, worketh for us a far more exceeding and eternal weight of glory; while we look not at the things which are seen, but at the things which are not seen: for the things which are seen are temporal; but the things which are not seen are eternal.* (2 Corinthians 4:16–18)

Here God is encouraging us to not lose heart because our present troubles won't last very long. When we take our focus off our temporary troubles and focus on the eternal, glorious experiences that God has for us, then we can persevere no matter how great the affliction.

Someday we may have the joy of sitting down with Matthew, Mark, Timothy, James, and Peter and asking them about some of their secrets of endurance and joyful perseverance. Until then, here are some thoughts that they wrote down to help us keep our focus where it should be.

> *But he that shall endure unto the end, the same shall be saved.* (Matthew 24:13)

> *And ye shall be hated of all men for my name's sake: but he that shall endure unto the end, the same shall be saved.* (Mark 13:13)

> *Therefore I endure all things for the elect's sakes, that they may also obtain the salvation which is in Christ Jesus with eternal glory.* (2 Timothy 2:10)

> *But call to remembrance the former days, in which, after ye were illuminated, ye endured a great fight of afflictions.* (Hebrews 10:32)

> *Blessed is the man that endureth temptation: for when he is tried, he shall receive the crown of life, which the Lord hath promised to them that love Him.* (James 1:12)

> *Behold, we count them happy which endure. Ye have heard of the patience of Job, and have seen the end of the Lord; that the Lord is very pitiful, and of tender mercy.* (James 5:11)

> *For what glory is it, if, when ye be buffeted for your faults, ye shall take it patiently? But if, when ye do well, and suffer for it, ye take it patiently, this is acceptable with God.* (1 Peter 2:20)

Continuing instant in prayer

Interestingly enough, to endure you must endure. To patiently endure under trials and troubles you must faithfully endure in prayer. How would you explain the difference between being devoted to prayer and dabbling in prayer? *The Complete Word Study Dictionary* edited by Spiros Zodhiates states that the original word for *continuing instant* (*pros-kartereo*) means to tarry or remain somewhere (Mark 3:9); to continue steadfastly with someone (Acts 8:13); to cleave faithfully to someone (Acts 10:7); referring to those who continually insist on something or stay close to someone (Romans 13:6).[1] Remember, "men ought always to pray, and not to faint" (Luke 18:1). "Continue in prayer, and watch in the same with thanksgiving" (Colossians 4:2). "Pray without ceasing" (1 Thessalonians 5:17).

When do you pray? How do you pray? Is your prayer life fervent? Are you consistent? Do you pray in faith believing that God will answer? Where is your prayer closet? Do you go to your closet and shut the door every day? Have you ever followed Jesus' example by getting up early (before light) and spending a season with your God in thanksgiving, praise, and adoration? I guess what I am trying to ask is, do you continue instant in prayer?

Do you rejoice in hope? Are you patient in tribulation? Do you continue instant in prayer? If you do, not only is God being pleased, and not only are you growing in grace, but you are demonstrating to God your thankful heart for His forgiveness and redemptive plan for your life. We can all say "amen" to such a joy.

CHAPTER 29

Give as God Has Given to You

Distributing to the necessity of saints; given to hospitality. *(Romans 12:13)*

Paul encouraged Timothy to encourage the "haves" to help the "have nots" by being willing to give. "Charge them that are rich in this world, that they be not highminded, nor trust in uncertain riches, but in the living God, who giveth us richly all things to enjoy; that they do good, that they be rich in good works, ready to distribute, willing to communicate" (1 Timothy 6:17–18). No one enjoys asking for money from others. The apostle Paul would make a wonderful modern day CFO with his exceptional understanding of both the complicated financial pictures and economic pressures on those who have dedicated their lives to serve Christ and His gospel. Those who are rich are not to be proud of their wealth or trust in their unreliable money (which could disappear by tomorrow). The rich are to trust God Who gave us all that we have in the first place. The rich should use their money for good, be generous to those in need, and always be ready to share with others. Do you tithe? Do you only tithe or do you give offerings also? What percentage of your income do you give back to God? How well do you share what God has shared with you? Do you have more than you need? Is there any possibility that God wants to supply the needs of others from the abundance that He has given you? Why do you have all that you have?

Distributing to the necessity of saints
- Share with God's people who are in need.
- Share what you have been given with those in need.
- Does God possibly want to supply the needs of His saints through you?

You cannot share *with* a person without sharing *in* a person's life. When you become a partner, you are "part of" that individual and his ministry. True sharing is never one sided. There is a partnership established and a mutual sharing understood. One may share the bucks and the other may share the blessings, but both are overjoyed by being used by God. Now, we have to study and learn how to discern a real need from a created crisis before we ever give. Make sure that what you are giving will be used for its intended purpose and that the gospel message is being heard because of your generosity.

If you were to counsel a young couple on how they should honor God with their giving, how would you counsel them? If you are not sure where to start, here are a few financial principles based on specific scriptural truths.
- Giving should be kept a secret between us and God (Matthew 6:1–4).
- Giving should be motivated by love and compassion (1 John 3:17).
- Giving should be cheerful (because we want to) and not grudging (because we have to) (2 Corinthians 9:7).
- Save in order to give. Always be ready when a true need arises (Proverbs 3:27–28).
- Give out of thanksgiving for what God has given to you (1 Chronicles 29:13–14).

- Give out of honor to God—not out of the surplus left over at the end of the month, but out of the abundance of the day after the paycheck is deposited (Proverbs 3:9–10).
- Remember God's promise to those who give but never allow the happiness of getting take precedence over the joy of giving (Luke 6:38).

Given to hospitality

What does it mean to be given to hospitality?

- Driven with dogged determination (given), show kindness to strangers (hospitality)
- Being eager to practice hospitality, desiring to open your home to whoever is in need
- Being willing to give of your comforts, your space, your personal zone to help those who are away from their own comforts, space, and personal zones
- Showing hospitality, not just when you are asked to, but eagerly go out of your way to offer it to others

Let your heart be the host for those who are hurting. Think about how you can fulfill Romans 12:13 on a regular basis.

Showing hospitality does have its trials and inconveniences. Benjamin Franklin said, "Fish and company stink after three days." Being hospitable to those who become fish-like is not always easy. Some friends, because of their short stay, keep unreasonable hours and rob the host family of much-needed rest. Others are snackaholics who come, empty the pantries, and move on to the snack cupboards of other unsuspecting friends. Some back up their tractor-trailers of troubles to your front door, dump a truckload of sorrows on your family, and leave! When you compare your initial response (what you *want* to say or do) with your godly heart's response (what you *should* say or do), you see how much growth you need in the art of hospitality. Remember what both Peter and his friend who wrote Hebrews remind us: "Use hospitality one to another without grudging" (1 Peter 4:9) and "Be not forgetful to entertain strangers: for thereby some have entertained angels unawares" (Hebrew 13:2).

Have you had any angels over for supper lately?

CHAPTER 30

Ask God to Bless Those Who Persecute You

Bless them which persecute you: bless, and curse not. *(Romans 12:14)*

Here God gives another short verse that is to the point and easily understood but, sad to say, often disregarded or defiantly disobeyed. There are only three words in this verse that have the possibility of being misunderstood: *bless*, *persecute*, and *curse*.

Bless them

The word *bless* comes from (*eulogeo*). The prefix *eu* means *good* or *well,* and *logos* means *word.* Together they mean "to speak well of." It is not merely saying nice things about those who curse you or curse your God, but it is asking God to put His blessing on them by doing His work of salvation and sanctification in their lives. If your enemies or persecutors knew Jesus Christ as their personal Savior or were walking with God, do you think they would be acting the same way toward you? Think of someone you have a difficulty with. Do you have them in your mind? Now look at them as they *would* be if they knew God and were walking close to God. In a few short words, describe the transformation of that person that just took place in your mind.

The concept of the word *bless* has been trivialized and cheapened to the point of its becoming simply a nice cliché. When someone sneezes, some say "God bless you." Many who don't even know God sing "God Bless America." In the southern U.S., the phrase "Bless your heart" is a nice way to say whatever you want about someone and still come across caring and kind. "Why he's as ugly as a bullfrog, bless his heart." "She's got the personality of a doorknob, bless her heart."

There are times when we can do or say something that becomes a real blessing to others: A twenty-dollar bill, a thank-you note, a cup of coffee, taking the time to go and pray for someone who is struggling, babysitting so a busy couple can go out on a date, washing someone's car, sharing the gospel, buying a bag of groceries, and the list goes on and on.

Be a blessing. If you need to bless those who persecute you, wouldn't you assume that you would also bless those who irritate you, provoke you, exasperate you, or ignore you? Is there anyone in your life right now who exasperates you? Rattles your cage? Drives you up a wall? Hounds you? Drives you to an insane asylum? How well is your "blesser" working?

Which persecute you

Do you ever feel persecuted, discriminated against, or bullied? People can be mean. Bullies are fearful people who seek out and attack those who are different from themselves. When I say "different," it could be a different race, a different religion, or a different political position. It could also mean a difference in the way they dress, they look, they think, they walk, or they live. It is sad that there are those in our world who ridicule and make fun of anyone or anything that is different. The ridicule that we might face today cannot even be compared with the persecution that the Roman Christians experienced in the first century. They were abused. They were beaten. They were tortured. They were killed. In our world, we can hardly imagine that. The Lord encouraged the ridiculed with words penned by both Matthew and Luke.

> *Blessed are they which are persecuted for righteousness' sake: for theirs is the kingdom of heaven. Blessed are ye, when men shall revile you, and persecute you, and shall say all manner of evil against you falsely, for my sake. Rejoice, and be exceeding glad: for great is your reward in heaven: for so persecuted they the prophets which were before you.* (Matthew 5:10–12)

> *Blessed are ye, when men shall hate you, and when they shall separate you from their company, and shall reproach you, and cast out your name as evil, for the Son of man's sake. Rejoice ye in that day, and leap for joy: for, behold, your reward is great in heaven: for in the like manner did their fathers unto the prophets.* (Luke 6:22–23)

Bless, and curse not

Just as the word *bless* means to call for God's favor to be poured out on an individual, so the word *curse* means to call for God's judgment to be poured out. Anyone who screams in anger for God to damn someone does not really know what he is saying. If they experienced five seconds in hell, they would never ask God to do that. The main reason you should bless and not curse is that your persecutor may someday be to you what Saul of Tarsus was to the first New Testament martyr Stephen. Can you imagine the conversation that could have taken place when Paul (formerly Saul) met up with Stephen in heaven? You can almost hear Paul asking for forgiveness and Stephen stopping him and saying, "Paul, it is okay! Since you were at my stoning you've been beaten, shipwrecked, hungry, lonely, imprisoned, tortured, and left for dead—and I've been in the presence of our wonderful Lord. It's okay, Paul—or should I say, *Brother* Paul."

After Sir Thomas More was tried and sentenced to death, his last words were, "My lords, I have but to say that, like as the blessed apostle St. Paul was present at the death of the martyr Stephen, keeping their clothes that stoned him, and yet be now both saints in heaven, and there shall continue friends for ever, so I trust, and shall therefore pray, that though your lordships have been on earth my judges, yet we may hereafter meet in heaven together, to our everlasting salvation."[1]

Wow.

CHAPTER 31

Rejoice and Weep with Others

Rejoice with them that do rejoice, and weep with them that weep. *(Romans 12:15)*

Rejoice with those who rejoice

What would hinder this simple command? Why would anyone *not* want to rejoice with someone who is rejoicing?

- Selfish focus: "No one rejoices with me!"
- Envy and jealousy: "Why do they get all the good stuff?"
- Critical and judgmental: "They probably stole it or begged for it!"
- Self-absorbed: "Why does God love them more than He does me?"

It always seems easier to weep with those who weep than to rejoice with those who rejoice. Why? Because it is not difficult to hurt for those who are experiencing something you hope and pray will never happen to you. But it is difficult to be happy and rejoice with someone who is blessed by God in a way that you have wanted to be blessed for years (and fear that you never will be). Think about it. Is it easier to console a friend who lost a job or congratulate a friend who was just hired (for the job that *you* applied for)? Is it easier to comfort a friend who just broke off an engagement or rejoice with a friend who just got married (to a person *you* dated in the past)? Our prayer needs to be, "Lord, teach me to be enthusiastically happy in my heart for others when You bless them in a way that I have been praying that You would bless me."

Weep with those who weep

How do people know when someone really cares? How do *we* know if we really care? In the day of Christ, professional mourners could be hired to come for a funeral—cry, mourn, weep, and wail—and then move on. It was all a professional show. Fake mourners would scream and tear their clothes, but they made sure they tore them on a seam so they could easily sew them up for future mourning opportunities. True "weeping with weepers" consists of a continued interest that seeks to help the afflicted through their many levels of grief. The Lord wept for Mary and Martha because of the loss of Lazarus, but then He (as God, of course) did something about relieving their grief. Paul is not asking for us to fake it as hired mourners, but to sincerely and honestly seek to feel the pain of others and hurt with them. You cannot manufacture tears on command. Tear ducts have their reservoir in the heart and can only flow when the heart is squeezed.

Believers who are hurting are part of your spiritual family.

So we, being many, are one body in Christ, and every one members one of another. (Romans 12:5)

God wants those who are hurting because of a crisis, difficulty, or tragedy to depend on Him for the grace to endure through it.

My brethren, have not the faith of our Lord Jesus Christ, the Lord of glory, with respect of persons. For if there come unto your assembly a man with a gold ring, in goodly apparel, and there come in also a poor man in vile raiment; and ye have respect to him that weareth the gay clothing, and say unto him, Sit thou here in a good place; and say to the poor,

Stand thou there, or sit here under my footstool: are ye not then partial in yourselves, and are become judges of evil thoughts? (James 2:1–4)

You may be next. How do you want others to comfort you when cancer, death, trials, or tragedies enter into your heart or home?

Brethren, if a man be overtaken in a fault, ye which are spiritual, restore such an one in the spirit of meekness; considering thyself, lest thou also be tempted. (Galatians 6:1)

As part of the loving family of God, you know that those hurting cannot expect sympathy from a cold and unfeeling world.

Seeing ye have purified your souls in obeying the truth through the Spirit unto unfeigned love of the brethren, see that ye love one another with a pure heart fervently. (1 Peter 1:22)

Who has ever been envious of trials, heartaches, and rejection?

How does it comfort your heart when others cry with you?

Now when Job's three friends heard of all this evil that was come upon him, they came every one from his own place: Eliphaz the Temanite, and Bildad the Shuhite, and Zophar the Naamathite; for they had made an appointment together to come to mourn with him and to comfort him. (Job 2:11)

It is sad that there are so few "weeping prophets" left.

Oh that my head were waters, and mine eyes a fountain of tears, that I might weep day and night for the slain of the daughter of my people! (Jeremiah 9:1)

Why should we think about how others feel before we focus on how we feel?

> *Remember them that are in bonds, as bound with them; and them which suffer adversity, as being yourselves also in the body.* (Hebrews 13:3)

When it comes to weeping, I am reminded of two very powerful words penned by the young apostle John, "Jesus wept" (John 11:35).

You can almost see the tears coming from the eyes of the Son of God when you read Christ's plea to Jerusalem.

> *O Jerusalem, Jerusalem, which killest the prophets, and stonest them that are sent unto thee; how often would I have gathered thy children together, as a hen doth gather her brood under her wings, and ye would not! Behold, your house is left unto you desolate: and verily I say unto you, Ye shall not see me, until the time come when ye shall say, Blessed is he that cometh in the name of the Lord.* (Luke 13:34–35)

Simply love others enough to truly rejoice with those who rejoice and genuinely weep with those who weep. God can give you the grace to love others in this way. He can!

CHAPTER 32

Humbly Enjoy the Company of ALL of God's Family

> Be of the same mind one toward another. Mind not high things, but condescend to men of low estate. Be not wise in your own conceits. *(Romans 12:16)*

How can I show my thankfulness to God for saving me from my terrible sin? In one word—humility. In one sentence—live in harmony with others and don't be so proud, haughty, or conceited that you can't enjoy hanging out with ordinary people!

Pride scares me. I know that I cannot live a godly, consistent Christian life without the grace of God. I also know that the only thing that would keep me from God's grace is my own stinking pride. God resists the proud and only gives grace to the humble. My treatment of others (even those that others would look down on) reveals my heart. Peter wrestled with pride but obviously had consistent victory in his latter years as he wrote these words.

> *Likewise, ye younger, submit yourselves unto the elder. Yea, all of you be subject one to another, and be clothed with humility: for God resisteth the proud, and giveth grace to the*

humble. Humble yourselves therefore under the mighty hand
of God, that He may exalt you in due time: casting all your
care upon Him; for He careth for you. (1 Peter 5:5–7)

Be of the same mind one toward another

Lovingly decide and unselfishly choose to think harmo-
niously with others—which includes those you work with,
those you go to school with, and those you live at home with.
To do this, you'll need to

- carefully consider their thoughts,
- understand them and know them well,
- refuse to deceive yourself that they have it out for you,
- realize that you cannot judge anyone's heart or motives,
  and
- know that just because you disagree with someone does
  not mean that either one of you is wrong, but that you
  each look at life from your own context, giftedness, and
  background.

Our humility-seeking journey through life seems to hit
some rough roads as we are confronted with difficult people,
selfish people, and non-thinking people. We are not the first
to struggle with others. Peter and Paul were often forced to
write confronting paragraphs in their letters to their believing
friends:

> *Finally, be ye all of one mind, having compassion one of an-*
> *other, love as brethren, be pitiful, be courteous.* (1 Peter 3:8)

> *Fulfil ye my joy, that ye be likeminded, having the same*
> *love, being of one accord, of one mind. Let nothing be done*
> *through strife or vainglory; but in lowliness of mind let each*
> *esteem other better than themselves.* (Philippians 2:2–3)

> *Now the God of patience and consolation grant you to be*
> *likeminded one toward another according to Christ Jesus:*
> *that ye may with one mind and one mouth glorify God,*
> *even the Father of our Lord Jesus Christ.* (Romans 15:5–6)

Mind not high things

If Paul were writing today, these verses might sound something like this. "Don't be a proud, arrogant know-it-all! Be willing to hang out with us lowly, ordinary people who may not be rich, good looking, or popular, but who may have much more to offer than you think. Don't think you are everything and others are nothing! Cultivate humility by letting the lowly lead your thinking." The words "mind not" are not a suggestion to consider, but a command to obey. Maybe you've heard a parent or a teacher say something like, "Mind you now!" or "You kids had better mind!" which is a nice way of saying, "Think!" This command tells us what *not* to think about. Stop thinking about yourself! Refuse to believe that you are some wonderful, great gift to mankind and that your work, school, or church probably would not be what it is without you. Don't be proud! God has a warning for those who are proud, haughty, and overbearing.

Only by pride cometh contention: but with the well advised is wisdom. (Proverbs 13:10)

Condescend to men of low estate

The word *condescend* has the idea of being carried or led away with or by someone or something. Normally we would hear a mom say, "All right now, don't get carried away!" But in this case, God is saying, "All right now, let's get carried away with lowly people and lowly tasks." What is lowly or insignificant in man's eyes may not be so lowly in God's eyes. Whether I preach to 150 or 1500, I should be "carried away" with the needs of either group. The 150 may seem lowly to those dealing with 1500; the 1500 is lowly to those filling stadiums with 15,000. Before you differentiate between the high and mighty and the poor and lowly, think about these words.

Come unto me, all ye that labour and are heavy laden, and I will give you rest. Take my yoke upon you, and learn of me; for I am meek and lowly in heart: and ye shall find rest

unto your souls. For my yoke is easy, and my burden is light.
(Matthew 11:28–30)

Be not wise in your own conceits

Never be conceited. Do not create the habit of being a know-it-all. Don't be full of yourself! Don't be blinded in your own eyes to who and what you really are before God (and before others). Those full of themselves have little room for anyone else. God says,

Seest thou a man wise in his own conceit? There is more hope of a fool than of him. (Proverbs 26:12)

If any man think that he knoweth anything, he knoweth nothing yet as he ought to know. But if any man love God, the same is known of him. (1 Corinthians 8:2–3)

The best antidote for a conceited, proud heart is a return visit to the cross. At Calvary, we are all sinners. Sinners are sinners. You may be an intelligent, rich, physically fit, and very successful sinner, but you are still a sinner. I don't want to ever forget what God has saved me from.

CHAPTER 33

Respect Others and Refuse to Retaliate for Any Reason

Recompense to no man evil for evil. Provide things honest in the sight of all men. *(Romans 12:17)*

Recompense

Refuse to pay back evil for evil to anyone. Respect what is right in the sight of all men by seriously thinking about what is honorable, right, and best in the eyes of everybody involved. In areas of revenge, retaliation, or expressions of bitterness, we are not to be debtors in any way. Is there anyone on earth that you wish you could make hurt as much as they have made you (or someone you love) hurt? How does true biblical forgiveness free you from such a desire to retaliate?

To no man

The "no way" phrase craze ("No way! Yes way!") has been around for some time. The Greek word *medeis* means "none, not any, no one, in no way, not even one." We are not obligated, or even encouraged, to play "gotcha-last" with words or actions towards others. But what about the guy that stole my iPod? *To no man.* But what about the girl that lied about me on Facebook? *To no man.* But what about my dad for what he did—and my mom for allowing it? *To no man.* "You're it. I quit!" does not make it in our grownup, mature world. (Or does it?) No man—regardless of what was said. No man—regardless of what was done. No man—regardless of how much it hurt. If anyone had the right to retaliate, it would have been our Lord Jesus Christ, and yet look at how He refused to retaliate.

> *For even hereunto were ye called: because Christ also suffered for us, leaving us an example, that ye should follow his steps: who did no sin, neither was guile found in his mouth: who, when he was reviled, reviled not again; when he suffered, he threatened not; but committed himself to him that judgeth righteously.* (1 Peter 2:21–23)

Evil for evil

Even though you have been the recipient of evil (bad, worthless, harmful, hurtful words, actions, or attitudes), you will never win by throwing the same back in their face. Giving back evil for evil results in an evil cycle that cannot stop unless someone refuses to retaliate. Someone has to stop! That someone is usually the one that allows God's grace to do a work in his or her heart. It is the someone who is open to God's replacing an unforgiving heart with a forgiving, patient, broken heart.

- "Only by pride cometh contention"—someone must stop! (Proverbs 13:10)
- "A soft answer turneth away wrath"—someone must stop! (Proverbs 15:1)
- "See that none render evil for evil"—someone must stop! (1 Thessalonians 5:15)
- "Recompense to no man evil for evil"—someone must stop! (Romans 12:17)

How do you stop? What is the key to ending such a vicious cycle? How would you counsel a friend who needed to stop retaliating?

God has the answer. The key to stopping (putting off) anything is to renew your mind (putting in) and start doing right (putting on).

Provide things honest in the sight of all men

Again, refuse to pay back evil for evil to anyone. Respect what is right in the sight of all men by seriously thinking about what is honorable, right, and best in the eyes of everybody involved. There is a mental process that we all go through when we totally disagree with someone. The word *provide* (*pronoeo*) comes from two words: *pro* ("before") and *noeo* ("to think"). In other words, we knew you were coming, and we are ready for you. We have not reacted, but through honest contemplation, we have acted accordingly. We have crawled into your shoes and attempted to see your side of the issue and understand why you think the way that you do. We want our attitudes and actions to be honorable, good, respectable, upright, admirable, worthy, principled, right. So even if we disagree with others, after spending serious mental energy looking through their eyes, we will have the calmness of spirit and confidence of our own view so that no one will respond in ugly, unkind, or mean-spirited words.

In the sight of all men

Interestingly, we have a "no way" starting Romans 12:17 and a "yes way" ending it: "to no man" and "to all men." No man should ever experience an evil word, a hurtful action, or a wicked attitude from any of us; all men should experience kind words, considerate actions, and honorable, loving attitudes from all of us. Even though we are to recompense to no man evil for evil, we should be attuned to repaying those who have impacted our lives in a positive way (parents, teachers, pastors, friends). Paul mentions this in his letter to Timothy as he deals with honoring widows. In 1 Timothy 5:4 he writes

"Let them learn first to shew piety at home, and to requite their parents: for that is good and acceptable before God." The word *requite* means to repay or to give back to those who have done so much for them. Children often forget what their parents do for them until they become parents—then they understand. Who needs a thank-you note or a love note from you today?

Obviously we are debtors to Christ for all He has sacrificed, paid, and given to us—we can never pay back that debt. Live your life in thanksgiving to God for His mercy.

CHAPTER 34

Live Peaceably with All Men (If It Is Possible)

If it be possible, as much as lieth in you, live peaceably with all men. *(Romans 12:18)*

No one can accuse Paul of being unbalanced. Living at peace with all men is not an easy task in a self-centered, self-focused, self-idolizing world. The phrase "as much as lieth in you" (so far as it depends on you) does put the responsibility on the mature Christian's shoulders. We need to do all we can! Your goal should be peace and not conflict. Your motivation should be nothing less than glorifying God by approaching others with a humble, loving, unselfish heart. So is this possible for you?

If it be possible

If, if in any way, reaching deeply inside of yourself, reaching as far as you possibly can, if you are able, if you are capable, if there is any way—live peaceably with all men. This phrase is both subjective and hypothetical. Paul is saying, "I am not saying that you can; I am not saying that others will ever allow it to happen; I am not saying that it is even possible to do so; but, as much as it depends on you, live peaceably with all men." What do you do when you are asked to do the impossible? How do you respond when someone asks something of you that you know is virtually inconceivable? Whenever I am asked to do the impossible, my mind races to three Bible principles that give us the biblical foundation for the comforting phrase, "I can't; but God can!"

For without [Jesus] ye can do nothing. (John 15:5)

I can do all things through Christ which strengtheneth me. (Philippians 4:13)

With men this is impossible; but with God all things are possible. (Matthew 19:26)

Interestingly enough, the root word for the words "it be possible" is *dunamai* which conveys the idea of being able, strong, and powerful—dynamite powerful. Since we cannot generate such power within ourselves, we know where this *dunamai* comes from, and so did Paul.

Finally, my brethren, be strong in the Lord, and in the power of His might. (Ephesians 6:10)

That He would grant you, according to the riches of His glory, to be strengthened with might by His Spirit in the inner man. (Ephesians 3:16)

Strengthened with all might, according to His glorious power, unto all patience and longsuffering with joyfulness. (Colossians 1:11)

Thou therefore, my son, be strong in the grace that is in Christ Jesus. (2 Timothy 2:1)

As much as lieth in you

The phrase literally means, "out of you". Dig into your heart of hearts and look for the grace, love, and patience that God put there. This peaceable living must come "out of you" and not out of anyone else. You are the one that must use the soft answer; you are the one that must drop the pride; you are the one that must stop pushing the issue. Out of you! The peace, if it is possible at all, depends on you. You must do your part and try.

Live peaceably with all men

Living peaceably is not always easy, but it is what God desires for us. Very few would want to build a new home, set up housekeeping, and raise their little ones in the middle of a war zone. If you had to be on guard 24/7, constantly waiting for the signal to grab your family and run to a bomb shelter, you would have a hard time being calm, at ease, or peace-filled in that environment. Too often we create our own war zones in our homes and churches. Such zones are complete with fighter-pilots targeting self-imagined enemies with contention, hostility, and conflict; tank-drivers aiming their gun barrels filled with clamor, malice, and hatred at disagreeing brothers; and foot-soldiers hoping to inflict fatal wounds with the chaotic, vengeful shrapnel from their hand-grenades that tear at those family members they are commanded to love but choose to hate.

History proves that people fear those who are different from themselves and fight those who disagree with them. Hindsight shows all of us that it is quite foolish to pick fights that neither party can win. Proverbs 18:6 reminds us that the fool's mouth calls for strokes, "Come on hit me! Hit me!" He picks fights with those that he does not understand. Why fight when you can be friends? At whatever point we are willing to honor and prefer others over ourselves, we will be on the way to living in peace instead of in strife.

When we esteem others highly, prefer others before ourselves, seek to edify each other, and allow God's peace to rule in our hearts, we have a much greater chance of living peaceably with all men. Don't hold a grudge; never refuse forgiveness; release offenses to God; seek to understand why others think the way they do; think no evil. Consider what it would be like if all were controlled by God's Spirit and unselfishly

living for God; then you can live peaceably with all men.
What does God promise to those who seek peace?

*Live in peace; and the God of love and peace shall be with
you.* (2 Corinthians 13:11)

Now that is a wonderful promise. God is simply saying,
"Believer, do you want to live and walk in my constant presence? Do this, please: live in peace."

CHAPTER 35

Let God Do His Just Work

Dearly beloved, avenge not yourselves, but rather give place unto wrath: for it is written, Vengeance is mine; I will repay, saith the Lord. Therefore if thine enemy hunger, feed him; if he thirst, give him drink: for in so doing thou shalt heap coals of fire on his head. *(Romans 12:19–20)*

Dearly beloved

Beloved, dearly loved, my dear friends, my beloved friends, I am on your side! I am your friend. What I am about to tell you is not because I am upset, hateful, or looking for ways to make you miserable. I am going to love you enough to give you the truth and give it straight. Ready?

- Dearly beloved, never take revenge.
- Dearly beloved, flee and run from idolatry.
- Dearly beloved, cleanse yourself from filthiness.
- Dearly beloved, I beg you to get right with each other.
- Dearly beloved, I fear you're in sin and won't repent.
- Dearly beloved, don't fear or be ashamed.

This is the first time in the New Testament that Paul uses the phrase "dearly beloved." These two words are rooted in *agape*, which denotes an unselfish love and concern for others rather than self. As we can see in the list of phrases above, each time Paul uses these words, he is getting ready to give a firm confrontation, rebuke, warning, or command as seen in Romans 12:19, 1 Corinthians 10:14, 2 Corinthians 7:1, Philippians 4:1, 2 Corinthians 12:19–20, and 2 Timothy 1:2, 8.

Avenge not yourselves, but rather give place unto wrath

Forgiveness is woven all through Romans 12:19–20. At the beginning of this study, we read these words: "As a sinner, I need forgiveness." Forgiveness is a promise (not a feeling) that my sin has been covered, dealt with, and forgiven so that it will not be brought up against me ever again. When God forgives, He justifies me. When God forgives, He declares me righteous. When God forgives, He frees me from the guilt and penalty of my sin. Is there anyone on earth (in your everyday life) that you refuse to forgive? Why is it so hard to forgive and let go of your vengeful feelings toward someone who hurt or offended you?

Remember, we are to forgive others in the same way that God has forgiven us (Ephesians 4:32). Forgiveness is not a feeling, but a promise. Forgiveness is not only a promise that we will not bring that sin up again, it is a release. We must release (let go of) our vengeful feelings toward those who sinned against us. Instead of trying to be the judge and the jury, we must let go of the situation (and the individual) and trust God to deal with them in His way and His time. Don't retaliate. Don't attempt to hurt others as much as they hurt you. Get out of the way and let God deal with it.

For it is written, Vengeance is mine; I will repay, saith the Lord

Just as God promises to forgive, He promises to judge sin. God is not only our loving Father but also our fearful Judge. Nahum, one of the Minor Prophets, reminds us that God is both a jealous God and One Who promises to take revenge.

> *The Lord revengeth, and is furious; the Lord will take vengeance on His adversaries, and He reserveth wrath for His enemies. The Lord is slow to anger, and great in power, and will not at all acquit the wicked [clear the guilty]. (Nahum 1:2–3)*

If you had the power, what would you do to punish someone you want to get back at? You might be able to hurt their reputation or embarrass them. Is that it? What would be your motive? Would your attempt to hurt them as much as they have hurt you and others result in sin itself? God not only knows what others have done and said, He knows the heart motive that precipitated such actions. God can do a better job than we can in passing judgment and choosing the just and proper punishment for the offender.

Therefore if thine enemy hunger, feed him; if he thirst, give him drink: for in so doing thou shalt heap coals of fire on his head

Since God is the One to take care of punishing others, you don't have to go there. Instead, you can go on the offensive and try to encourage others. You may never change the consequences of God's vengeance in their eternity, but you will never be blamed for it because of your acts of kindness while on earth. If your enemy is hungry, feed him! If those who hate you are thirsty, give them something to drink! Hunger and thirst are basic needs without which death is the ultimate consequence. Paul is not talking about making their life comfortable or sending them out to gorge on an all-you-can-eat buffet, but treating with kindness those who will die if they don't eat or drink. Those who have attacked you and sought to destroy everything you stand for may be in huge need someday. When the cancer comes, the tragedy takes place, or the sudden death of a loved one shocks your enemy, your love and kindness would be the least expected, but the most impacting thing that the enemy may experience. Look at it this way, how would you treat a thirsty dog or horse? How do you treat your plants? Are dogs, horses, and azaleas more important than people to you? What could such acts of love and kindness do for those who have made your life miserable?

There have been many explanations and illustrations of the phrase "for in so doing you shall heap coals of fire on his head," but the simplest meaning is to excite in him feelings of painful regret. Maybe if the offender knew God or lived for God, he would not have treated you in such a way.

Forgive, and simply let God do His just work.

CHAPTER 36

Overcome Evil with Good

Be not overcome of evil, but overcome evil with good. *(Romans 12:21)*

Don't let evil conquer you, get the best of you, or defeat you. Conquer evil by doing good, get the best of evil by doing good, and defeat evil by doing good. Do good!

Be

Be something, be anything, be, be being. If life (like driving) were controlled by stoplights, *be* would be the green light. In life, don't apathetically sit as if you are at a red light doing nothing or going nowhere. Apathy loathes being! Don't apprehensively hang out at a yellow light living in fear or virtual paralysis. Apprehension fears being! What if I fail? What if people laugh at me? What if I get my feelings hurt? Be careful but not fearful! Go for the green light and be actively pursuing life. Keep moving, keep doing, and keep being. If you had to rate your spiritual life by a stoplight color (red for apathy, yellow for apprehension, or green for action), what color would you choose?

Be not

Negative! No way! "Read my lips. Not gonna do it!" NOT! Learn to be negative in a positive way. If someone tempts you to sin, simply say "No, thank you." Learning when to say "no" in life can save your heart from tons of hurt.

Be not overcome

The Greek word for overcome is *nikao*, which means *victory*—to be victorious, prevail, conquer, subdue, defeat, triumph over, overpower, overthrow, to win! "Nike-ized" Christians are overcomers who refuse to be overcome. In the Olympic wrestling world, overcomers do not allow themselves to get pinned down on the mat. They may get knocked down (or even knocked out), but they will get back on the mat and keep on fighting. Overcomers never give up! What does it take to overcome you? What keeps you from being victorious (*nikao*) in your daily devotions? What keeps you from being victorious (*nikao*) in your thought life? What keeps you from being victorious (*nikao*) in your battle with anger or fear?

Be not overcome of evil

How do you know if you are overcome of evil? If your thought life is out of control and you consistently give in to lustful thoughts, you are being controlled by lust. If you can entertain yourself with sensual movies, TV, or Internet sites that are sexually explicit but do not bother you, you have been conquered by lust. In other words, you are being overcome of evil.

How do you know if you are overcome of evil? If you can scream at your parents or your kids and not humbly ask them to forgive you, you are controlled by anger. If you won't talk to some friends because they make you so mad, you have been conquered by anger. In other words, you are being overcome of evil.

How do you know if you are overcome of evil? If you cannot say "no" to friends, no matter what they are asking, you are controlled by fear. If you want so badly to be accepted that you start talking, acting, and thinking like evil friends, you have been overcome of fear. In other words, you are being overcome of evil.

Be not overcome of evil, but overcome evil with good

Be victorious over evil; prevail over evil; conquer evil; subdue evil; defeat evil; triumph over evil; overpower evil; win over evil! How? God will give the grace (the power and the desire), and in this case He tells us what weapon to use. Choose your weapons! A gun? A knife? A lead pipe (in the library with Professor Plum)? How about *good*—that which is good is profitable, useful, excellent, distinguished, upright, top quality, and beneficial? What is good for now is good forever! What is good in God's eyes should be good in my eyes. What good is there in fear, anger, or lust? How are they profitable for eternity? How are they useful for today? How are they excellent for tomorrow? God has much to say about being overcomers, and if you are like me, even after a long study of Romans 12, I still have so much to learn about over-coming evil with good.

> *For whatsoever is born of God overcometh the world: and this is the victory that overcometh the world, even our faith. Who is he that overcometh the world, but he that believeth that Jesus is the Son of God?* (1 John 5:4–5)

> *Ye are of God, little children, and have overcome them: because greater is he that is in you, than he that is in the world.* (1 John 4:4)

> *Be not overcome of evil, but overcome evil with good.* (Romans 12:21)

Closing Thoughts

Well, time has flown by and we are at the end of our study. It is good to be reminded of some thoughts from the beginning of our study.

How many things does a person have to know to live and die a happy, contented, fulfilled life? Bible scholars and Bible students have wrestled with this question for centuries, and the general consensus seems to be only three: (1) how great are my miseries and sin; (2) how I can be delivered from my misery and sin; and (3) how I am to be thankful to God for such deliverance.

When Paul wrote the word *therefore* he was not just giving a general glimpse of the three hundred fifteen verses of Romans 1–11, but specifically man's complete ruin in sin (Romans 1–3) and God's perfect remedy in Christ (4–11). Knowing what we were and what God has done, should it not impact the way we live each day?

Strong Bible teaching should always be accompanied by solid Bible application. Doctrine without application could give us big heads and little hearts. Application without doctrine could result in full hearts and empty heads.

It is not difficult to understand the extreme wickedness of our own hearts, but to clearly explain what God has done for us and why He would treat such wicked sinners with such love? Now things get difficult. The end of Romans 11 reveals to us how untraceable and unsearchable God's deliverance, mercy, and grace to us really are.

I trust you have enjoyed your study of Romans 1–12 and learned many ways that you can say "Thank You!" to such a wonderful God Who has done so much for you. Live your life thanking God for what He has done for you. There are hundreds of ways to thank God, and we have skimmed only twenty-four of them from Romans 12.

How can you show your gratitude to God for what He has done for you?

- Understand Paul's *therefore* (Romans 12:1–2)
- Understand God's mercies (Romans 12:1–2)
- Understand sacrificial living (Romans 12:1–2)
- Understand worldly conformity (Romans 12:1–2)
- Understand God's transformation (Romans 12:1–2)
- Understand God's will (Romans 12:1–2)
- Think! Think! Think! (Romans 12: 3)
- Accept who you are (Romans 12: 4–5)
- Love one another (Romans 12: 4–5)
- Thank God for His grace gifts (Romans 12:6–8)
- Use your gifts for God (Romans 12:6–8)
- Encourage others, give to others, and lead others in a merciful way (Romans 12:6–8)
- Practice genuine love (Romans 12:9)
- Love and honor others (Romans 12:10)
- Serve God with an enthusiastic, fervent attitude (Romans 12:11)
- Patiently rejoice and continually pray (Romans 12:12)
- Give as God has given to you (Romans 12:13)
- Ask God to bless those who persecute you (Romans 12:14)
- Love others so much that you can rejoice and weep with them (Romans 12:15)
- Humbly enjoy the company of all—*all*—of God's family (Romans 12:16)
- Respect others and refuse to retaliate for any reason (Romans 12:17)

- Live peaceably with all men (if it is possible) (Romans 12:18)
- Forgive. Don't retaliate. Let God do His just work (Romans 12: 19–20)
- Overcome evil with good! (Romans 12: 21)

Overwhelmed with what God has done for me,
Rand Hummel

Endnotes

CHAPTER 1
1. Warren W. Wiersbe, *The Bible Exposition Commentary: New Testament*, Vol. 1 (Wheaton: Victor Books, 1989), PC Study Bible 4.

CHAPTER 7
1. *American Heritage Dictionary*, 4th ed., s.v. "justify."

CHAPTER 8
1. Ibid.

CHAPTER 12
1. Wiersbe.

CHAPTER 13
1. Donald Grey Barnhouse, *Expositions of Bible Doctrines: Taking the Epistle to the Romans as a Point of Departure*, Vol. 4 (Grand Rapids: Eerdmans, 1977), PC Study Bible 4.

2. Warren W. Wiersbe, *Be Right : An Expository Study of Romans* (Wheaton: Victor Books, 1977), PC Study Bible 4.

3. William Hendriksen, *New Testament Commentary: Exposition of Romans* (Grand Rapids: Baker Book House, 1953), PC Study Bible 4.

4. Joseph Hall, *The Works of the Right Reverend Joseph Hall* (Oxford: Oxford University Press, 1863), PC Study Bible 4.

CHAPTER 14
1. Spiros Zodhiates, ed., *Complete Word Study Dictionary of the New Testament* (Chattanooga: AMG Publishers, 1991), PC Study Bible 4.

2. Horst Balz and Gerhard Schneider, *Exegetical Dictionary of the New Testament* (Grand Rapids: Eerdmans, 1990), PC Study Bible 4.

CHAPTER 15
1. Zodhiates.

2. Joseph Henry Thayer, Carl L.W. Grimm, and Christian Gottlob Wilke, *Thayer's Greek Lexicon of the New Testament* (Grand Rapids: Zondervan, 1970), PC Study Bible 4.

3. Ibid.

4. Adam Clarke, *Adam Clarke's Commentary* (Electronic database: 2006) PC Study Bible 4.

CHAPTER 17
1. Hendriksen.

CHAPTER 19
1. Barnhouse.

CHAPTER 23
1. Barnhouse.

CHAPTER 28
1. Zodhiates.

CHAPTER 30
1. Joseph S. Exell, *The Biblical Illustrator: New Testament* Volumes (London: 1887), PC Study Bible 4.